GUILDFORD
REMEMBER WHEN

GUILDFORD
REMEMBER WHEN

David Rose and Bernard Parke

Surrey Advertiser

breedon **books**
PUBLISHING

First published in Great Britain in 2007 by
The Breedon Books Publishing Company Limited
Breedon House, 3 The Parker Centre, Derby, DE21 4SZ.

ISBN 978-1-85983-588-3

Printed and bound by Antony Rowe Ltd. Chippenham, Wiltshire.

CONTENTS

INTRODUCTION

'I FIND that the further I go back, the better things were, whether they happened or not.'

Those words, by the writer, satirist and humourist Mark Twain, may ring true for some, but there is no escaping the fact that in today's fast-moving world it is enjoyable to take some time out and reflect on our past.

Over the last 60-odd years Guildford has seen many changes. Whether life was better just before World War Two, during it, or in the decades that followed, is, of course, open to debate. But on one level, *Guildford Remember When* gives the reader the opportunity to revisit the town during those times and challenge their own thoughts on the subject.

On another level, this snapshot of everyday life will hopefully interest those who want to know more about Guildford's recent history.

Beginning with a look at how Guildfordians lived through the period covered in this book, including the town during wartime, how people dressed, the post-war housing shortage, healthcare, motoring and the celebrations of Queen Elizabeth's coronation in 1953, the book moves on to reflect on what it was like to grow up during those times.

Pastimes and other leisure activities such as youth clubs, cycle speedway, the cinema and theatres, are focused on; followed by a chapter tracing the histories of some of the local businesses operating at that time such as Drummond Bros, Victory Industries, Plastic Coatings and the Friary Meux brewery.

Guildford's metamorphosis from a medium-sized market town to a regional centre is looked at by way of plans made towards the end of World War Two, the building of the cathedral, buildings that have disappeared and a look at the shops and businesses that were once in North Street.

Many interesting and influential people have lived and worked in Guildford. Here, we take a look at a select few who made their mark in the decades before and after World War Two. Some of those from Guildford who lost their lives fighting for their country are remembered, along with a look back at the time of National Service.

The final chapter contains some of the stories that hit the local (and national) headlines a few decades ago. Who remembers the train crash of 1953, the Queen's visit in 1957, the cruel winter of 1962–63 and the floods of 1968?

This book would not have been possible without the help of a number of people who, over a number of years, have either loaned pictures for copying, passed on snippets of information, or have given help and advice about Guildford in years gone by. Drawing on this archive of information has been most useful to the authors as they have written and compiled this book in recent months.

In no particular order, thanks go to: Tony Blanchard, Ivy Glass, Mick Downs, Douglas Graham, Doris Butler, Josie Roker, Brenda Liddle, Ron and Jannett Down, Dorothy Parker, Avril Plumridge, Dennis and Pat Lavery, Linda Davis, John and Brenda Wakefield, Ann Tizzard, Age Concern Guildford for the photographs taken by the late F.C. Saunders, Stan and June Newman, Ronald Heathorn, Marie Kyte, Sheila Atkinson, Jean Douthwaite, J. Grindel, Judy Wilmott, Jill Chittleburgh, Tony Reardon, Peter Gardiner, Rosemary Povey, Bea Killick, G. Rogers, Dennis Flack, David Bennett, Keith Gates, Mick Douglas, David Brice, Phillip Goodhand-Tait, Nigel Enever, Ken Howes, John Phillips, Jim Poulter, Harold and Rae Barber, former Guildford Cathedral archivist Bob Ellison, John Young for the photographs taken by the late Elsa Megson, Minnie Grover, Mary Bishop, Bill Bellerby, Kathleen Webster, David Oakley, Brian Holt, David Clarke, Stan Wickham, John Corpus, Matthew Alexander of Guildford Museum, the Rt Hon. Lord Vinson, John Theobald, Douglas Barnes, John Glanfield, Frank Phillipson, Alderman John Woodhatch, Ron Shettle, John Mansfield, Christine Johnson, Alma Scholfield, Claude Kauffmann, Peter Black, Clive Taylor, Jeanette Porter, Kathleen Woodward (photograph of the Revd Walter Boulton), Joy Christopher, Roland Sidwell of Guildford Guildhall, David Tribe, Jean White, Sylvia Lagden, Elizabeth Ball and Claude Wilkins.

Sincere apologies to anyone not mentioned whose photographs have been included.

David Rose and Bernard Parke

April 2007

CHAPTER ONE

LIFE BACK THEN

Before World War Two

If you could step back in time to Guildford in the years just before World War Two, you would see a good deal of change taking place.

The borough boundary had been extended in 1933 as areas to the north of the town were developed for housing. The population at the outbreak of the war was 40,870.

Guide books in the late 1930s, although waxing lyrical about Surrey's charming county town and its many historic features, could not help but acknowledge the changes that were taking place. The 1938 edition of *The King's England, Surrey*, by Arthur Mee, noted: 'Guildford has nearly doubled itself in size since 1900, and is now not only climbing the Hog's Back, but climbing the hills in various directions, even ascending close to St Martha's.'

Guildford High Street bedecked with flags and bunting to mark the Silver Jubilee of King George V in 1935. This was perhaps the town's biggest celebration in a difficult decade with many economic hardships.

The 9th Guildford Scout Troop's float in the carnival that celebrated the Silver Jubilee in 1935.

The old market town of Guildford that had served the local agricultural community for many years was indeed changing and expanding. The town's major employer, Dennis Bros, had brought in many workers to make its specialist vehicles. The construction of the A3 bypass had also seen an influx of people – many from parts of the UK such as the North East and South Wales, where there was, during the depression of the 1930s, mass unemployment. A number of these remained after the road was completed and sought work in the light manufacturing industries in the area or perhaps in the local construction industry.

The mainline rail link to London was electrified in 1937, which meant that Guildford was an ideal place to live for those who sought to earn their 'daily bread' commuting to and from the capital. A daily third-class return ticket to Waterloo cost three shillings and ninepence, and first-class cost five shillings and ninepence.

By 1939, the borough of Guildford covered 7,184 acres. There were 861 acres of parks and pleasure grounds. The rates were set at 10 shillings in the pound, with one shilling in the pound for water. Shops in the town closed early on Wednesdays and the cattle market was on Tuesdays.

The borough's official guide was upbeat in promoting the town's many benefits to its current residents and to those who might have been looking to move to Guildford. In the guide's foreword, the then well-known writer and local resident, Eric Parker, wrote: 'Guildford's communications by road and rail are all that a county's town could be.' However, the guide was also keen to point out that the town had practically no congested areas and that there were three large car parks near the town centre, with 'several others in convenient sites'. Bus services, it noted, were good too.

The guide stated that Guildford was a healthy town and it went on to champion those benefits that included an excellent sanitary system and pure water supply, with an average death-rate lower than that for the rest of Surrey.

For electricity, Guildford was the second–cheapest town in England and it also had a plentiful supply of gas. 'The shops are decidedly good,' the guide boasted, 'and prices are kept down to reasonable rates'. It noted that delivery services were provided by several large London stores and that all the big banks had branches in the High Street.

Of permanent open spaces and upmarket housing, the guide commented: 'Merrow Downs, Stoke Park and Pewley Down provide wide open spaces in the immediate neighbourhood of the town, to which have recently been added the Chantries and Shalford Park. Most of the better residences are on high ground such as the slope leading up to the well-known Merrow Downs, Warwick's Bench, facing Chantry Woods, and Guildown.'

World War Two put a halt to Guildford's housing expansion, but its population continued to rise. By August 1940, it was up to 49,700, but it had dropped back to 47,000 by the end of the war.

Guildford Lido and the bypass, seen top left, were two major building projects that took place in the town during the 1930s. The county town was expanding at this time and there was an influx of people from more depressed parts of Britain.

THE NEW LIDO, GUILDFORD

The town expanded with new housing estates in the 1930s. Roads were laid and existing ones repaired with tar spraying and road-brushing machines like this one made by F.G. Barnes at its Ockford Engineering Works in Godalming.

The sharp increase was due to a number of factors. These included evacuees coming from London to escape the Blitz, and the doubling of Dennis Bros' wartime workforce to 3,000. Plus there were further workers who found employment with other local firms engaged in the war effort, and those clerical staff who made Guildford their temporary home when their London companies relocated here after suffering bomb damage.

Guildfordians soon became acquainted with these newcomers; and it wasn't just mums and their kids mixing with their counterparts from the East End of London. Factory workers (men and women) were making friends, and perhaps relationships, with new colleagues; and then, of course, there were visitors from the other side of the Atlantic. The area around Guildford was soon to be filled with Canadian soldiers who lived in camps within the Surrey Hills, while their officers commandeered any spare large houses. They came to defend the UK from a ground attack, should Hitler have ordered an invasion. The first wave of Canadians alone numbered some 23,000.

There were Americans stationed in the South East as well, but it is the Canadians who were most numerous in and around the Guildford area. When off duty, they were regular visitors to the town and its pubs. They may have been liked by some of the local girls, but there was sometimes friction between these often tough characters, from places such as British Columbia and Nova Scotia, and local Guildford lads.

Guildford was taking on a completely different look.

On the Home Front

Few people in Guildford could have been surprised when the news broke on Sunday 3 September 1939 that Britain was at war with Germany. There was no panic, everyone appeared calm and a spirit of quiet determination prevailed.

The town had been preparing for the inevitable for some time. Details of air-raid precautions (ARP) had been circulated to local authorities in 1935, and in April 1937 the Air Raid Wardens' Service had been set up. In September 1938, the ARP service was mobilised. Volunteer wardens were drawn from responsible members of the public. Chosen to be a leader and an adviser to their neighbours in a small area or a street, their tasks were to ensure that there were adequate air-raid shelters within the area they covered, and once war was declared to enforce the night-time blackout of homes. This meant regular patrols; and if they spotted a house or premises where a shutter or blackout curtain had not been drawn properly, the familiar cry of 'put that light out' would be heard. There were fines for those caught not complying, and in Guildford local magistrates were kept busy. On one occasion alone, in September 1939, 14 people were summoned before the bench. In fact, eight of these were road users (five being cyclists). Each fine was about five shillings. However, as the war progressed and the situation became more serious, those caught infringing the blackout were fined between £1 and £3.

Air-raid wardens wore blue serge uniforms with overcoats, berets and

In 1941, the then Home Secretary and Minister of Home Security, Herbert Morrison, visited the town. He is pictured here (right) in Woodbridge Road with the then Mayor, Alderman Vernon Wilkinson (centre). The Home Secretary reviewed Civil Defence personnel and opened a nursery school in Westborough.

Wartime local newspaper advertisement placed by White's store explaining its position regarding air raids during opening hours.

boots. Their black steel helmets had a large white 'W' painted on them.

Should a bomb fall in a warden's sector, his or her job was to inform their control office and keep the public inside their shelters updated with details of the raid. Wardens had the job of putting out small fires – a stirrup pump and a bucket of water, or sand, was commonly used – rescuing inhabitants, giving first-aid and helping those whose houses had been destroyed to the nearest rest centre.

Some householders with cellars had them reinforced to be used in times of an air-raid, while others bought prefabricated shelters that they erected in their gardens. These came in various forms, the Anderson shelter being perhaps the most popular. To make it blast proof, the entrance did not lead directly into the shelter, but turned at a 90-degree angle.

One particular model, made of concrete, was called the Squad. The standard version cost £14, or £15 for a more deluxe model. They were made by Burbidge Builders Ltd, who were based in East Horsley, and could be bought from Angel, Son & Gray, in Woodbridge Road.

Morrison shelters were used inside the home – usually in the middle of the sitting room.

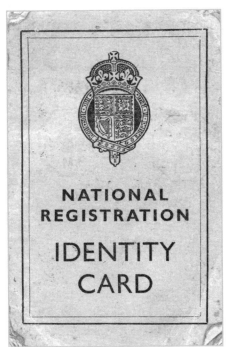

Those that did not have a shelter, indoors or out, would take refuge in the cupboard beneath the stairs when an air raid was on.

Guildford had a number of public air-raid shelters. They included trenches in Foxenden Quarry, the Borough Hall, the Playhouse Arcade, the Angel Hotel, Ward Street Hall, the public baths in Castle Street, the glass works in Portsmouth Road, the former technical institute in Park Street, the Castle Grounds, Onslow Street car park, the cattle market car park, and at Station Meadows. Dennis Bros motorworks had its own shelters.

However, from the outbreak of war until the summer of 1940, the feared enemy planes did not come. The period became known as the Phoney War, but Guildford was experiencing wartime events and activities that were completely new to the town.

National Registration Identity Card.

The printers, Billings & Sons, based in Walnut Tree Close, had its own fire brigade made up of men and women. They are pictured here in the autumn of 1944.

In the plans for the evacuation of people at risk from enemy bombings, Guildford had been classified as a reception area as it was not deemed a priority target. On Friday 1 September 1939, two days before war was declared, Guildford began to receive children and some adults from danger areas. On that day alone – a day that thousands of children across the whole country were on the move – Guildford received 2,109 children and 259 adults. Of this total, 1,423 were billeted in the borough and 945 in the rural district. On the next day, 1,161 children and 738 adults arrived. And of these, 970 found lodging in the borough and 929 in the rural area. On the Sunday, Guildford took in a further 111 children and 51 adults. The borough found accommodation for 128 of these, while the rural district housed 34.

The majority had come from London by rail, but among the total, London Transport buses brought 115 expectant mothers to Guildford. By the Sunday afternoon, when these often bewildered children were sitting down to tea for the first time with their new 'guardians' and trying to come to terms with where they were, the local authorities and those involved in the evacuation process were breathing a huge sigh of relief that the whole operation had run so smoothly.

However, by the end of 1939, some children had gone back home to their parents simply because the bombs were not yet falling. For some, the strain of living away from their parents was too great. Also, less well-off parents and those busy with war work were finding the journeys down to Guildford to see their children at weekends difficult.

Number 22 Leas Road pictured after bombs hit numbers 17 to 29 on the night of 27 September 1940.

Another view of the bomb damage in Leas Road.

In July 1940, Guildford received a number of children who had been evacuated from the Brighton area. Three trains brought them and they were then taken to 12 billeting centres (mostly schools) where they were registered and given refreshments before being taken to the places where they were to stay. Most of them went to live with families in villages surrounding Guildford such as Send, Ripley, Wisley, the Clandons, the Horsleys, Peaslake, Shere, Gomshall and Shalford, among others.

Problems of strangers cohabiting with each other were inevitable. A Guildford couple were accused of ordering a London woman out of their home contrary to the billeting order. Guildford Borough Police Court heard that a dispute had arisen about the state of the room the woman, her husband and 19-year-old daughter had occupied, for which they paid the householders 17 shillings a week. The woman had also got into arrears over the payment and a heated exchange took place. The court heard that the evacuees were on the verge of departing anyway and it was all something of a misunderstanding. The summons was dismissed.

In August 1941, the *Surrey Advertiser* printed a story titled 'Advice to Evacuees'. It read: 'When evacuees residing at Woodbridge Hill appeared in a summons and cross-summons, they were all bound over at Guildford Police Court. It was stated that there had been considerable trouble between the two families.

'The Mayor (Alderman V.G. Wilkinson) said it was up to evacuees to make life as tolerable as possible for each other. He hoped these family quarrels would stop.

'"You are getting yourselves a bad name in the district," he said, "and if this sort of thing goes on, we shall have to take other steps. People are not used to these troubles in Guildford. We hope you will agree among yourselves a little better in the future".'

Bullet holes, believed to have been made by a German aircraft, can still be seen in the brickwork of the County School in Farnham Road.

Officers from Stoughton Barracks were also billeted with local families, although their stay would not usually be for long.

There were, however, evacuees who remained in Guildford for most of the war. In a letter published in the *Surrey Advertiser* on 14 July 1945, a D.N. Griffiths wrote on behalf of the staff and pupils of the Wandsworth Technical Institute, thanking 'our friends in Guildford for the uniform kindness which has been so generously given to us during our evacuation.

'From the time of our arrival in Guildford we have received unbounded hospitality and assistance. The governors of the Guildford Technical College willingly placed the available facilities of the college at our disposal, and we have at all times received every support from Dr Ward and his staff.

'The provision of billets for a school of 450 boys and girls was a considerable task, but this was successfully overcome throughout our long stay of nearly six years'.

The letter concluded: 'We are leaving Guildford with considerable regret, and feel sure that the personal friendships which have been formed will be maintained in the future.'

Guildford came face to face with the horrors of the war going on in Europe when, in late May 1940, many of the trains carrying British and French troops evacuated from Dunkirk passed through the station.

Germany's *blitzkrieg* (lightning war) had ripped through France and, by 24 May, with British troops cut off, it was decided to evacuate as many of the men as possible through the port of Dunkirk. Hundreds of boats, both large and small, sailed from England to rescue them and, by 4 June, a total of 338,000 soldiers had been brought back from France. Britain's four main railway companies provided 186 10-coach trains to take the weary and injured men to destination points across the country.

On payment of sixpence, to help raise funds for Guildford's 'Warship Week' in 1942, people could get the feel of what the inside of an aircraft gun turret was like.

With reporting restrictions in place, the *Surrey*

The Mayor, Alderman Vernon Wilkinson, takes a look inside the gun turret.

Three young boys get to grips with a Bren gun at a wartime exhibition held at the Borough Hall. The exhibition was staged to raise awareness of fuel economy.

Advertiser wrote: 'Trains full of men, tired and unshaven, yet in the best of spirits despite the grim ordeal of battle, have passed through various parts of the south this week.

'Many hundreds of civilians have watched their progress with pride and sympathy, and at least in one Surrey town this feeling has been translated into a practical expression by local members of the WVS [Women's Voluntary Service] and other helpers actuated by a similar motive.'

The town was, of course, Guildford. Many volunteered to hand out refreshments to the soldiers while their trains paused at Guildford railway station over the weekend of the Dunkirk evacuation. The Red Cross and Salvation Army were among other organisations in Guildford who went to help.

The *Surrey Advertiser* reported: 'As each train steams into the station these helpers are ready with great jugs of tea, baskets of cakes, packets of cigarettes, and other kinds of refreshments, together with boxes of postcards for writing home to relatives, and these are handed out to the men as they crowd to the compartment windows. The postcards are afterwards collected and posted, and if the money is available, telegrams are also dispatched. The postcards being sent in bulk, are sent post free.

'Kisses were exchanged, hands waved, and hats swung in the air. As the train disappeared in the distance, there came a brief silence, a silence that had a note of pathos, and then cups and other utensils were collected, and preparations made for the next arrival.'

Another story in the *Surrey Advertiser* appeared under the heading 'Wounded arrive – some with burns from blazing oil'. It stated that these soldiers, 215 in number and mostly French, were taken to 'hospitals in the county'. These were the Royal Surrey County and St Luke's hospitals. The Guildford branch of St John Ambulance transferred the men in a fleet of ambulances and buses. In fact, the brigade was kept extremely busy throughout the war, attending accidents and bomb incidents in the area, taking injured people to hospital and administering first-aid.

The late summer of 1940 not only witnessed the Battle of Britain, in which the RAF bravely repelled the Luftwaffe, but also the start of Hitler's order for his planes to bomb non-military targets. As the bombing of London began, soon to be called the Blitz, the lives of Guildfordians, along with those in other towns and villages, were disrupted as air-raid sirens sounded and terror was brought by the noise of aircraft overhead.

Guildford Borough Council's 'bomb incident record' lists some 74 reported incidents of high explosive, incendiary, thermalite, oil-drum and flying bombs falling within the borough. The first incident was on 16 August 1940, in which a bomb was reported to have fallen in the Mount Cemetery. The last was on 28 August 1944, when a V1 (or doodlebug) landed in Aldersey Road. The majority of bombs fell during the autumn of 1940 and on into the start of 1941– a time when the Blitz was at its height. The final five incidents were all V1s, the first of which fell in a field to the west of Foxburrows Avenue, on 28 June 1944.

It is believed that seven people in Guildford lost their lives as a result of enemy bombs during the war. The first three deaths were on Monday 14 October 1940 when a bomb destroyed two houses in Rydes Avenue. They were Ronald Mower, Louisa Moore and Elizabeth Burgess. Six other people were injured. On 12 May 1941, bombs were dropped on Charlotteville. Eyewitnesses said they identified a Dornier, litup by searchlights, as the aircraft that dropped one bomb in Addison Road and two in Cline Road, one of which killed Herbert Walter Washington. The final V1 that fell on Aldersey Road claimed three lives. They were Dorothy Ackland, who was a resident at number 12 (the house on which the bomb fell); Alice Poynter, who lived next door; and Sylvia Mary Preston, who lived with her husband Arthur, also at number 12, and who died of injuries in the Royal Surrey County Hospital a few days later.

A fair number of bombs that fell in the borough were away from built-up areas, but properties were also damaged in Onslow Village and near the town centre in Leas Road. At the latter, some considerable amount of damage was done. The date was 27 September 1940.

At the time, and for years after for that matter, Guildfordians often said that the bombs which fell on the town were simply from aircraft who had missed their targets, or were jettisoned by aircrews who were hastily making their way back home. But it is possible that the bombs that fell on Onslow Village may have been intended for nearby Henley Fort, which the Germans may have thought was a military target, although it was a Home Guard post.

More sinister is the line of bombs that fell across the town at the time of the Leas Road incident. Studying the council's official 'bomb map', they appear to have been intended for the Dennis Bros factory. It is still rumoured that one of the bombs fell into the River Wey near Walnut Tree Close; it did not explode and has never been found!

A frightening daytime raid on Wednesday 16 December 1942 was witnessed by many people. Believed to have been another Dornier, the aircraft attempted to spray the railway station with bullets. However, it seems likely that the gunner could not get his sights quite right and a hail of bullets hit the Royal Surrey County Hospital and the County School, both in Farnham Road. Bullet holes, thought to have been the result of this attack, can still be seen in the brickwork of the County School to this day. No one appears to have been badly injured, but children from Guildford Park

Home Guardsmen who worked for the Post Office in Guildford. They are pictured near Haydon Place.

School in Ludlow Road saw the aircraft very clearly as they ran from their classrooms across the playground to the air-raid shelters.

The aircraft then appears to have headed south and dropped two bombs, one of which hit a train enroute from Guildford to Horsham as it approached Bramley station. Four years after the attack the *Surrey Times* of 21 December 1946 recalled the event and stated that eight people were killed – three outright and five others either on their way to hospital or after admission. About 40 other passengers were injured.

The Local Defence Volunteers (LDV) was launched on 14 May 1940 as a fighting force to guard every town, city and village in Britain. Mostly made up of men who were too old to join the armed forces or younger men in reserved occupations, in Guildford 1,000 men came forward within the first three days, reporting to the borough police station in North Street. By July, the organisation had changed its name to the Home Guard.

The 4th (Guildford) Battalion Surrey Home Guard was eventually made up of seven general duty companies (A to F) with a factory guard (G). It was led by Colonel Guy Westland Geddes, who had retired to Guildford in 1934 after a distinguished military career. Guildford's 'Dad's Army' went on night-time patrols, manned road blocks and guarded potential enemy targets such as the waterworks and electricity works. In September 1944, once the end of the war in Europe was in sight, the Home Guard was stood down. On 4 December of that year men of the Guildford Home Guard took part in a final parade in the grounds of the technical college.

A physical feature that was hastily constructed across southern England in 1940, which included

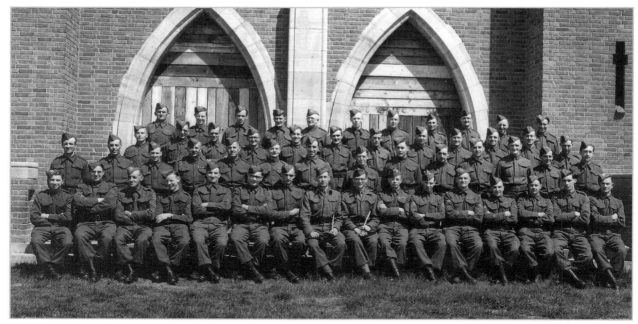

Pictured in front of the then unfinished cathedral are Home Guardsmen who worked for Drummond Bros during World War Two.

concrete pillboxes, tank traps and deep ditches, was known as the GHQ Stopline. It passed through Guildford roughly along the line of the Greensand ridge to the south of the town. Should Operation Sealion, the English name for Hitler's invasion plan, have taken place, this line might well have been the final defence the enemy would have encountered as they swept towards London. A number of pillboxes and anti-tank traps (also known as dragon's teeth) are still in place within the Guildford area. However, there is no trace today of the defence ditch, incorporating a number of rifle and machine-gun pits, that was dug across Stoke Park.

Life on the Home Front was not easy, especially when it came to putting food on the table.

In 1940, butter, bacon and sugar were rationed. People had to make do with meals consisting of vegetables, with a small amount of meat. As the war went on, more foods were added to the ration, and to supplement these many people grew their own vegetables. Of the many campaigns initiated by the Government, perhaps the Dig for Victory campaign is most remembered.

In Guildford, allotment gardens sprang up all over the town, with hitherto uncultivated land turned over to the growing of vegetables and other crops.

Pig, poultry and rabbit clubs began to flourish along with the Guildford Allotment and Gardens Association, the latter being formed in 1943. At the time there were 1,000 allotments in the borough.

British Restaurants allowed people to buy a wholesome meal without giving up precious ration coupons. The first British Restaurants to open in Guildford were in October 1940 when the Mission Church Hall in Westborough and Stoughton Church Room opened their doors. Others opened in the upper High Street; Addison Road, Charlotteville; and Merrow Village Hall. Meal tickets were issued that took the form of coloured cellulose acetate tokens in the shape of coins, and these were presented in exchange for a subsidised meal. Typically, a meal would consist of soup, roast beef with Yorkshire pudding, potatoes and cabbage, with apple pie and custard and a cup of tea, and would cost one shilling. The tokens were issued in the restaurant in return for cash, with individual colours denoting the meal courses and beverages the diner had chosen.

The restaurants were run by the council and were supported by organisations such as the WVS. The one in the upper High Street could serve up to 600 meals at lunchtimes. People were encouraged to eat in such restaurants to save fuel, lighting and time.

Guildfordians dug deep into their pockets throughout the war each time there was an appeal for funds to equip the armed services. For example, within a week in 1940, the town's Spitfire fund had raised £2,500. War Weapons Week, also in 1940, raised a massive £250,000. Although local firms

Local firms engaged in war work took part in a procession through the town as part of the Guildford War Work Week, from 29 September to 4 October 1941. These women worked for Dennis Bros.

Some of the girls who worked for RFD in Stoke Road. The firm made sea rescue equipment for the war effort.

and wealthy individuals chipped in the greater amount, ordinary people of all ages did their bit too, through a variety of schemes. Warship Week in 1942 raised £573,000 and the town was able to adopt HMS *Lively*. The town gave its name to a Churchill tank after the Guildford Rural District Savings Committee was a winner in the Summer Savings Campaign in 1942. Other national fundraising events that the town took part in included Wings for Victory Week and Salute the Soldier Week.

Factories in the borough of Guildford played no small part in helping the war effort by producing a range of items. Dennis Bros, with its works at Woodbridge, was by far the largest factory, employing up to 3,000 people. With shifts working around the clock, the factory turned out about 7,000 trailer pumps for the fire service and armed forces, 700 Churchill tanks, 3,000 of its Dennis Max trucks, 1,500 of its three-ton trucks, 1,000 30cwt trucks, 3,000 tracked armoured vehicles, several million small parts for aircraft, as well as thousands of bombs and bomb tails. A complete workshop was given over to the manufacture, assembly and testing of a special heavy-duty gearbox, giving five forward and five reverse speeds; this was supplied for use in tanks such as the Comet, Cromwell and Centaur. The works manager, Mr A.W. Hallpike, could certainly be proud of the diversity of output!

Other local factories engaged in the war effort included the electrical engineering firm of Nelco at Shalford, which made components for the Royal Navy; RFD, with factories in Guildford and Godalming, making sea rescue equipment; Warner Engineering on the bypass near the fire station; and Vokes at Normandy, making filtration equipment.

Hard-working local people needed a break from time to time, but with travel generally restricted and most traditional seaside locations out of bounds anyway, not to mention money being tight, there were few opportunities available. Therefore, stay-at-home holiday activities were organised. The *Surrey Advertiser* of 1

IMPORTANT NOTICE
TO ALL
SAFEGUARD PASSENGERS

On and after next Monday, January 4th, and until further notice the LAST BUS to WESTBOROUGH will leave at 9 p.m., and our LAST BUS to DENNISVILLE will leave at 8.45 p.m.

No Sunday Services will operate on Sunday MORNINGS. The FIRST BUS to WEST-BOROUGH will leave at 1 p.m. and our FIRST BUS from DENNISVILLE will leave at 1.30 p.m.

Local newspaper advertisement from 1943 issued by the Safeguard Bus Company.

August 1942 reported that the holiday fortnight began with a successful sports meeting on the Sports Ground, in which the civil defence, youth organisations and members of the forces were among those taking part, with a large crowd going to watch. There were also concerts; other sporting events such as boxing, cricket and tennis; rabbit shows; games for children and baby shows.

In its edition of 8 August, the *Surrey Advertiser* noted: 'Children have enjoyed themselves "up to the hilt", and it has been no uncommon sight to see 1,000 of the little ones at attractions for their special benefit.

'Seventeen children from Ramsgate, Guildford's "adopted" town, have been guests of the Guildford youth organisations and the Rotary and Round Table clubs, and have been in a camp at the corporation's site at the Chantries.'

The newspaper estimated that between 5,000 and 6,000 people visited Stoke Park on one day alone, and 2,000 took part in a swimming gala at the lido.

However, the town had to wait until the middle of 1945, with the end of hostilities in Europe and then the unconditional surrender of Japan, before celebrating peace.

VE Day on 8 May 1945 saw a two-day holiday. Across the borough of Guildford there were street parties and a youth rally victory parade in the High Street. Sunday 13 May was observed as a day of national thanksgiving. There was a special service at Holy Trinity Cathedral Church.

The adults of the Tilehouse Estate, off Worplesdon Road, pose with their sandwiches, cakes and washing before their VE Day party in May 1945.

Residents of Grantley Gardens, off Woodbridge Hill, celebrate VE Day.

More smiling faces, young and old, on the Tilehouse Estate, this time for their VJ Day party in August 1945.

The end of World War Two was marked with VJ Day on 15 August, and again there were two days of holidays with more street parties. Floodlights lit up the town after dark and dancing went on in the High Street well into the night. Bonfires were lit and, for a time at least, people forgot about the hard times they had endured.

Many aspects of life on the Home Front would never be forgotten. For women, these included working out the weekly shop with the family's ration books and then the long queues outside shops. Many people were engaged in voluntary fire watching. The roof of the *Surrey Advertiser* offices in Martyr Road was one such place, and a room with beds and food-making facilities was provided.

Double Summer Time was introduced to make the most of daylight and so lengthen the working day, and in doing so save power. To the man in the street it meant daylight almost to midnight, but resulted in absolute hell for children. At the time youngsters were told the rhyme: 'Early to bed and early to rise makes Jack healthy, wealthy and wise.'

Wartime slogans such as 'Make Do And Mend' and 'Keep Mum, She's Not So Dumb,' can hardly be forgotten, nor perhaps the sight of hundreds of military vehicles in the Guildford area in the build-up to D-Day in 1944. For others, the view from high ground, such as on Pewley Down, and looking to the northern sky glowing red as London was in the grip of the Blitz, won't have been forgotten. Girls of the Land Army were a common sight working on local farms, as were Italian prisoners of war from the camp at Merrow Down out on working parties, clearing ditches by the roadside.

Some people never forgot the day when two Mustang aircraft collided and crashed in Stoke Park, killing both pilots. The date was Saturday 17 April 1943. One young eyewitness at the time recalled: 'Suddenly, there was a dull thud and a burst of what looked like steam as two of the aircraft collided. It seemed so unreal, as if it had happened in one of the Disney cartoons showing at the Guildford Playhouse.

'What was perhaps more striking were the indentations in the grass made by the bodies of the airmen who had no time to use their parachutes. It is sad to recall, but we as children just accepted this crash as normal life. I suppose that was the life we lived in those dark days.'

Shops and rationing

Running a small shop was especially hard for grocers in the days of food rationing, which was introduced during the War and continued afterwards.

Profit margins were cut, while competition was rife. Nearly every street had at least one small shop, while some roads, such as Manor Road in Stoughton, had at least four grocery shops within a few hundred yards.

Customers could only buy their rations from one shop. However, once a year they could re-register at another shop if they wished to change.

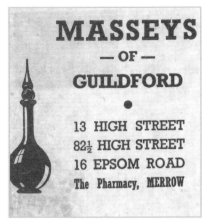 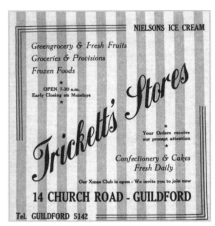 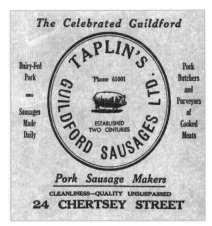

Paper bags from three long-gone Guildford shops. Masseys the pharmacist, Tricketts' Stores and Taplin's Guildford Sausages Ltd.

This time of re-registering was particularly traumatic for the grocer, who had no power over these moves. He would only know from the Ministry of Food how many of his customers had left him for another trader.

Coupons had to be cut from the customer's ration book at the time of purchase and counted and balanced each month, before being sent to the local Ministry of Food office.

Butter in the war years was particularly scarce and many parents gave their entire butter ration to their children and made do with the Government's issue of margarine, which tasted like axle grease! It bore no resemblance to today's spreads, and to eat this wartime 'grease' was enough to put anyone off margarine for life.

In the upmarket grocery shops, such as Sainsbury's in the High Street, butter was crafted by assistants in white aprons as perhaps sculptors would work; but in their case they used two large butter pats to eke out the meagre ration.

Cheese was equally crafted from large, rounded, barrel-like blocks, which were covered in a protective rind.

The sliced loaf made its appearance in the early 1950s, with only one grocer in a given district allowed to stock it.

A firm called Nevilles supplied sliced loaves, with a daily delivery to Guildford from its bakery at Acton. However, things became more relaxed when Wonderloaf entered the local market.

These were not the only suppliers who would make daily trips to the borough of Guildford. Doubledays, the pie-maker from Brixton, was also very popular with Guildfordians.

Bananas did not reappear until 1947, while oranges were almost unheard of at that time. When they did finally arrive, in their distinctive wooden crates, the greengrocer Ernest Nicholls, of Worplesdon Road, sold them one at a time to his customers.

Mr Nicholls ran an open-fronted shop with his wife. He was a fat, jovial little man, clothed in a large horizontally-striped apron.

He sold off the unwanted orange crates for firewood. Sometimes boys were allowed to turn these crates into go-carts, with the addition of four old pram wheels.

Butchers' shops were also plentiful. In the Stoughton area alone there were three such shops to choose from. Horace Dyer was at the top of Manor Road, Sparrow's was in Barrack Road and Austin's was on Woodbridge Hill. All were within striking distance of each other, but competition between them was not as keen as it was with the grocery shops.

Corned beef was frequently seen on ration. Children seemed to find this more palatable than the tough meat that would appear on the table at meal times. Sausages were also popular, and the lack of meat in them would be made up by using bread. One of the best sausage shops was Taplin's, in Chertsey Street.

Apart from homemade varieties, preserves or jams were not available during the depths of food rationing. There was a strawberry jam substitute, to which were added small wooden-style pips to make it look more like the real thing.

Woolton Pie was promoted by the wartime cabinet. It consisted of carrots, parsnips, potatoes and turnips in oatmeal, with a pastry or potato crust and served with brown gravy. Needless to say, this

Looking down Woodbridge Hill with its row of small shops. The Guildford Stores can be seen on the corner of Weston Road and next to it is Austin's the butcher.

meat-free pie was not popular. It got its name from the then Minister of Food, Frederick James Marquis, 1st Earl of Woolton.

Early on during the war, there was a glut of carrots. It was said that RAF pilots ate them to improve their night vision. This ploy rumour was started to hide the fact that it was our invention of radar that was helping them navigate in the dark. The musical comedians of the day helped with this ruse by saying that it must be true because you would never see a rabbit wearing spectacles!

Meat or fish paste was in common use for sandwiches, and was washed down by the tea ration. Coffee was hardly ever available, and few people drank it back then, except perhaps Camp coffee, made from chicory.

Most cakes were handmade, but only if the ingredients could be purchased. Many people kept a few chickens or rabbits to eat. The roosters would be fattened up for special occasions such as Christmas. Eggs from the hens would be pickled for later use.

The only apples available were grown in the UK and were therefore a seasonal crop. Children delighted in the sport of 'apple scrumping' from local gardens. But eating too many unripe apples led to frequent trips to the lavatory!

Dedicated followers of fashion

The war years meant a period of make do and mend. All garments were rationed and children's clothes were no exception. They were handed down from child to child with little regard as to whether they were a good fit. The question was whether they kept the child warm and dry.

Even shoes were handed down from generation to generation. Consequently, they hardly ever fitted the next wearer properly, so there was much discomfort, not to mention damage to young growing feet.

Sports wear was of the pre-war vintage. However, swimwear was sometimes knitted by mothers or aunts. But when wet they looked rather indecent, as the garments sagged badly.

Those children who wore a uniform to school had to wear it for Sunday best as well – mainly because rationing prevented parents buying any other 'best' clothes.

The main school outfitter was Stan Hardy, who had shops in Friary Street and High Street. It sold uniforms to parents whose boys went to the Royal Grammar School. Messers Kinch & Lack in the High Street and Harry Newell of H.A. Newell & Son in North Street were other suppliers.

Boys who went to state schools did not generally wear a specific uniform, but wore a school cap. Boys wore short trousers for at least 14 summers in the belief that the longer that knees were exposed to fresh air, the stronger they became. Anyone wearing long trousers before that age would be branded an outcast, and even worse, a sissy! Needless to say, bare knees became badly cut and grazed. It was unusual to see a boy without scabs on his legs from some long-forgotten game.

Members of Stoke Youth Club, seen here wearing some classic 1950s fashions during their production of *On Stage Please*.

With few homes centrally heated, it was necessary to wear thick underclothes. These same garments were worn in summer as well as in winter. Much discomfort was caused if there was a particularly hot spell.

During the war years 'austerity wear' ruled the world of ladies' clothing. To save on fabric, pleats in dresses were not allowed. When 'utility wear' was introduced, just two pleats were permitted.

Skirts were worn at about knee length, also to save on material. Women on war work wore blue overalls, known as factory clothes. Their hair was normally worn under a head scarf.

A favourite ploy was to take an old stocking and to roll it into a ring. This would be placed on the head and the hair curled over it. When working with machinery no loose hair was allowed, for obvious reasons.

Stockings were scarce. Nylons were not in general use until after the war, although the American servicemen were usually able to supply them to their new-found English girlfriends.

Women often dyed their legs with tea leaves to give the impression of wearing stockings. A line

Youngsters from Ardmore Avenue, Stoughton, in typical childrenswear of the 1940s. Some of the boys are even wearing ties on what appears to be a play day!

would be carefully drawn up the calf of the leg with an eyebrow pencil where the stocking seam would usually be found.

When the war ended, more material became available and as such hem lines were dropped to just below the calf. This was known as the 'new look'.

For men, the post-war years saw the time of the 'Burton suit'. It could be bought from Burton's store in Guildford High Street. The alternatives were suits from John Collyer, the 'thirty shilling tailors' in Friary Street; or perhaps Hepworths. These suits were, in general, very good value, but the seams were quite scant. They had a tendency to split in the most embarrassing places.

The 1950s was the time of an innovative raincoat, made possible by the more general use of plastic. It was called the pack-a-mac.

Head wear was recommended. The slogan was 'If you want to get ahead, get a hat'. Dunns in the

Day trippers pictured at the seaside in front of a Rackcliffe's of Guildford coach. The photograph is a good example of what older people wore in the post-war years.

Fashion advertisements from local newspapers during the 1940s and 1950s for William Harvey, the Guildford & District Co-operative Society, and Rego.

High Street sold fashionable hats. Popular ones were those similar to Bavarian hats with feathers.

The bowler, however, was a badge of office for the more senior professional sector. However, they seemed to lose popularity after the jazz musician Acker Bilk took to wearing one on stage. But for some years after, a bowler hat was kept in a particular bank office for any manager who was called upon to visit Harrods in London on business.

Acute housing shortage and the prefabs

Many families in Guildford yearned for a home of their own after the war. For scores of ordinary working people, actually buying a property didn't even come into the equation – for them there were none available anyway.

Fed up with living with in-laws or in a rented room, some families took desperate steps and occupied once grand homes that had become empty, while others moved into vacated army huts. They became squatters, and for a while, at least, the council had no option but to let them remain there.

By 1946, many servicemen had returned home – some for the first time in over six years. There were plenty of young married couples, and, like today, their main aim was to find a home. There had also been many wartime marriages of haste, and these couples were also having to readjust to a very different world.

Stoke Hill Mansion used to house homeless families.

In Guildford, the borough council was doing its best to provide more homes. In 1944, the council had bought Stoke Hill Mansion and its 184-acre estate for £42,000. Although it had built some council houses there already – known as Paynter's Close, after the family that had owned the estate – it had plans to develop the whole area, which it had renamed Bellfields. However, building materials were in short supply and so was skilled labour. Building work started on 1 January 1946, but it took several years for all the houses to be completed.

The borough council had a strict council house waiting list, with homes being granted to people who earned points across a number of categories.

For about 10 years from 1948, huts at the former prisoner of war camp at Merrow Down were used for emergency housing. A strong community was forged there and although families eventually moved to permanent homes, many lifelong friendships were made.

The *Surrey Times* of 13 July 1946 ran a headline: 'First tenants at Bellfields. Envy of 4,000 applicants.' It wrote: 'Tenants for the first pair of houses completed for Guildford Corporation since the war have been selected and one family is already settling into their new home.'

The two families had been chosen by the tenants selection sub-committee. The committee worked from case numbers and did not know the identity of those whose points tally they were adding up. The couple with the highest number of points was a Mr and Mrs J.H. Desborough, who, with their two children, had been living in a single furnished room in Nightingale Road.

Nissen-type huts were converted for temporary housing at Merrow Woods. These were also in use until the end of the 1950s. There was just one telephone in one of the homes that had to be shared by all the 60-odd families living there. Seen here are Percy and Winifred Shrubb, who, with their daughter Pat, lived there at the end of the 1950s.

Their tally was 452 points and was arrived at in the following way:

Applicant married, 40 points.

Daughter aged 10, 10 points.

Son aged five, 5 points.

Expectant mother, 5 points.

Applicant employed in Guildford, 100 points.

Resident in Guildford (1 point for each year), husband and wife combined, 20 points.

Exceptional ill-heath of one child, 75 points.

Living in furnished room, 45 points.

Each child under 21, (10 each) 20 points.

Overcrowding, 45 points.

Husband's overseas service with forces (1 point each month), 22 points.

Joint use of kitchen, bathroom, lavatory and with no separate meters, 65 points.

The Desboroughs were, in fact, not the first family to move in. Their new neighbours, Mr and Mrs C.H. Lee, with a son and two daughters, occupied their new home a couple of days before. Their tally was 442 points. The newspaper report noted that Mr Lee was a baker and had served in the Royal Navy.

The houses had been built under contract by a Mr C.C. Yeates and the council. Unfortunately, neither the *Surrey Times*, nor the *Surrey Advertiser* in its report, gave the exact road name and number of the pair of houses. The former did state that the Lees' home had been the showhouse on the site and that 6,000 visitors had taken a look inside prior to it being occupied.

The report concluded by stating that of the 4,000 applicants for council homes, only 30 had more than 400 points. The chairman of the tenants selection sub-committee, Alderman Vernon Wilkinson, believed there would be 250 permanent homes ready at Bellfields by the end of 1946.

Although these rare photographs have no captions written on the reverse, they appear to show the roads being laid and possibly the foundations being constructed for the prefab homes at the far end of Westborough.

Alderman Wilkinson had more good news when he announced at the same time that Guildford's first pre-fabricated houses (prefabs) would be arriving for assembly within a few days on a site in Westborough. It was estimated that 100 would be erected within about a month and the foundations had already been laid for them.

On 13 August 1946, the *Surrey Times* reported Alderman Wilkinson as saying that his committee had anticipated providing homes to applicants on 360 points by the time the 100 prefabs had been let. However, since the first two brick-built homes at Bellfields had been let there had been a surge of fresh applicants. Others, already on the list, had come forward stating that, as they were now employed within the borough, they wanted their tally recalculated. He added that following the publicity given to the first Bellfields tenants, there had been endless trouble at the re-housing department office with criticisms, recriminations and angry comments directed at the staff. He stated that the points system was being adhered to strictly, but human nature being what it is, there were bound to be some inequalities that were unforeseen.

In less than a month, some families, frustrated at not being able to find a home of their own, became squatters, occupying a number of unused buildings across the borough. A former army camp at Stoke Hill, off the Woking Road, was the first location. The *Surrey Times* of 7 September

Once the prefabs in Westborough had been occupied another close-knit community quickly developed. Mums were delighted to have a fitted kitchen with an electric cooker, electric copper and a fridge.

Prefabs, like this one in Park Barn, were rather cold in winter, but at least the bathroom had hot running water.

1946 stated that the camp, 'formerly used by Pioneers, is now a bustling little colony'.

It added: 'Most of the squatters are pitifully short of furniture, as they have been living in rooms. None seemed resigned to making the camp a permanent home, and the Corporation and Army officials, who have visited them, while sympathetic, have not been able to give definitive information as to their future.

'There is electric light and water in the camp – the wash-house and showers and wash benches having a hot-water boiler. A row of nine flush lavatories requires boarding for mixed use. The squatters are prepared to face the hardships which must be theirs with the coming of winter, though they feel doubtful of making the improvements themselves.'

The first person to move in told the newspaper that he had found one of the huts unlocked, so

The living room of a prefab that has been restored and fitted with 1950s furnishings at the Rural Life Centre at Tilford, near Farnham.

best use of redundant materials. They should also make minimal use of timber and bricks and use the Government-approved 'heart unit' of back-to-back kitchen and bathroom plumbing. As far as possible, factory-made parts were to be used, and the design was to be easy to assemble on site, while making minimal use of traditional skills.

The Westborough prefabs appear to have been of the aluminium type, known as the B2. These were designed by the Aircraft Industries Research Organisation for Housing. There just happened to be surplus capacity in aluminium production after the war and these were the first homes in the UK to be manufactured on a production line.

The B2 became the most common type of prefab in the UK with 54,000 built, but at £1,160 each, they were the most expensive. They were not as robust as other types made of asbesto-cement sheets.

The prefabs in Guildford lasted slightly longer than the given 15-year life expectancy. In March 1965, the *Guildford & Godalming Times* reported that the council hoped to demolish the prefabs by 1967. However, their tenants, who had been offered new permanent council homes at Slyfield Green, were in a dilemma. They feared they might lose the sympathy of the housing department if they did not take up the offer made to them. But the prefabs were comfortable and they liked Park Barn too.

The parade of shops in Stoughton Road, Bellfields, in the days when the estate was new.

43

Prefabs were indeed luxurious compared to the standard of accommodation many people had come from. Housewives were delighted to have a fitted kitchen complete with electric cooker, electric copper and a fridge. And there was a bathroom with hot running water, and fitted wardrobes. A great sense of community sprang up too. Children happily played with one another and neighbours became friends as gardens were planted up and tended.

The restored prefab that can be found at the Rural Life Centre in Tilford is a delight to visit. It has been fitted out with period furniture and fittings. Step inside and you can almost feel that you have stepped back in time.

Healthcare

Healthcare in the post-war years in Guildford was centred around its two hospitals, the Royal Surrey, then in Farnham Road, and St Luke's Hospital in Warren Road. There was also the Jarvis maternity unit in Stoughton Road and people with mental illnesses were cared for at nearby Brookwood Hospital. Local GPs operated from practices, many of which are still with us today, albeit now in newer surgeries.

The National Health Service (NHS) was formed in 1948, to provide healthcare for all citizens based on need, not the ability to pay. It brought hospital services, family practitioner services (doctors, pharmacists, opticians and dentists) and community-based services into one organisation for the first time. Funding was a problem back then and nurses could often be seen rattling collection tins on street corners.

Children suffered from what were then regarded as normal illness that unfortunately formed a part of growing up. These included mumps, chicken pox and measles.

Nursing staff out fundraising for the Friends of Guildford Hospitals.

Poliomyelitis (infantile paralyses, or polio) was a crippling disease and was not really controlled until the Salk vaccine arrived from the USA in 1959.

It was quite normal for children to have their tonsils removed as a matter of course for health reasons. Children recovering from the operation would often be given ice cream – a rare treat in those days.

The first two decades of the NHS saw a number of changes following various Government reports. Management structures were gradually improved along with advances in healthcare.

Nurses from the Royal Surrey County Hospital in their distinctive uniforms in the late 1950s.

The Salmon report of 1967 detailed recommendations for developing the senior nursing staff structure and the status of the profession in hospital management.

The last of the old-style matrons to be appointed at the Royal Surrey was Susan Underdown, who took up her post in 1964. She commanded authority, but was not at all like the matrons portrayed in the *Carry On* films.

She became known as the matron with the smile, which was the result of a finely honed career. Matron Underdown had spent 12 years as a ward sister, night sister and administration sister at the Royal Free Hospital in London. She then took a personnel management course at King Edward's Staff College, London. She returned to nursing at the Bristol Royal Hospital as an assistant matron, before coming to the 250-bed Royal Surrey.

Matron Underdown did not believe in 'eating and sleeping' nursing, as many did. Once her working day was over, she made sure she changed into casual clothes to relax. She encouraged her staff to follow her example and to pursue outside interests. This, she believed, prevented people from becoming petty-minded by being too close to their vocation.

Dr Robert Bingham McMillan was a well-known medical superintendent at St Luke's Hospital in the 1950s and 1960s. He was a rather outspoken character who said that caring for the chronically

Dr Paddy Boulter lights a Christmas pudding on Albert Ward at the Royal Surrey County Hospital in Farnham Road in 1967. Standing to his left is Ward Sister Pam Hobson, later to become Sister Pam Parke.

sick was a major British industry. However, Dr McMillan knew that without a good deal of extra funding, it would be no easy task. He also said that Britain had had its health service on the cheap.

He did not share the view of those taxpayers who were outraged that overseas patients were coming to the UK for free treatment. He based his arguments on the story of the Good Samaritan – believing it our Christian duty to care for all, no matter what creed, colour or race.

When he came to St Luke's Hospital in 1947, there were plans to replace the old hospital buildings with a modern million-pound hospital. It was to be Dr McMillan's job to supervise the work. However, due to a change of NHS policy, the new hospital was never authorised.

Dr McMillan pioneered the first day hospital for the elderly in the UK at St Luke's. He believed that loneliness in old age led to mental deterioration and also thought that no one should have to travel more than five miles to attend their local day hospital.

The 1960s fundraising scheme to install a Betatron radiotherapy machine to fight cancer included Dr McMillan on its executive committee.

The machine, which had been developed in Switzerland, was to be the first of its kind in the UK. More than £200,000 was raised through public subscription over an intense two-year period to pay for it. It was an amazing effort by local people. Money poured in from young and old, and rich and

poor alike. The highlight of the fundraising campaign was a gala film night at the Odeon cinema. The guest of honour was a new young mother, Princess Alexandra.

The Betatron, with its massive 35 million electron volts, was able to concentrate and focus more efficiently on the areas of the body affected. To prevent the escape of radiation, the building the Betatron was housed in

Entrance to St Luke's Hospital in Warren Road.

required 1,000 cubic yards of concrete. Steel rods used in its construction, if laid end to end, would have stretched 44 miles and weighed about 50 tons. The walls in the main treatment area were eight feet thick. The unit had a suite of rooms and in the waiting area there was a piece of sculpture by Franta Belsky. He was a president of the Society of Portrait Sculptors, and a former cancer patient.

Guildford's union workhouse had once been on the the St Luke's site. Its infirmary was later known as Warren Road Hospital. In 1945, it was

The Betatron building at St Luke's Hospital.

renamed St Luke's, after the tin chapel in nearby Addison Road. In 1991, following the expansion of the current Royal Surrey County Hospital (opened in 1980), it and St Luke's merged to become a single NHS trust. Services, wards and departments moved to the Egerton Road site, making the Warren Road site redundant. It has now been redeveloped for housing.

One local GP, whose career spanned the era before and after the NHS, was Dr Gordon Cranstoun, who practised from his home at Perry Hill Lodge in Worplesdon from 1922. In his early days he did his rounds on a Douglas motorbike and sidecar. Born in Shropshire, Dr Cranstoun believed that in many cases a physical condition had its roots in marital difficulties.

In 1928, he moved his practice to a row of cottages that had been converted to a proper surgery and doctor's house. It was opposite Worplesdon Place. Cranny, as he was known, did his rounds over a large area to the north of Guildford. At the surgery, his wife answered the phone and was the receptionist. He carried on single-handedly during the war years, but gratefully took on a partner, Dr John Moir, in 1946.

On the right road

Those lucky enough to own a car in the 1940s were mostly running patched-up pre-war models that were both overweight and underpowered.

More often than not, owners pushed them out of their garages at weekends to clean them – mainly for the benefit of on-looking neighbours.

Cars were licensed quarterly in those days, and the summer quarter was the most popular. Many vehicles were left mothballed in the garage for the rest of the year.

A report from 1954 stated: 'Car holders do little winter driving and in the spring feel the urge to tinker with the family saloon to get it in tip-top trim for the open road, as the beautiful British countryside begins to beckon and the magic carpet of motoring starts to unfold.'

A collection of cars in for servicing and repairs at Jackson's Garage off the High Street.

The budget of that year was said to be disappointing, as there was still a purchase tax of 50 percent on cars. Petrol was also expensive.

The price at the pumps rose to four shillings and sixpence per gallon. However, for a time the owner of the Markenfield Garage, on the corner of Markenfield and Woodbridge Road, was offering unbranded petrol at five gallons for £1.

Mechanic Fred Tedder works on an Austin at Jackson's Garage.

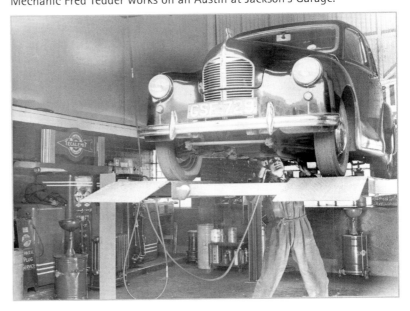

Some drivers tried to update their cars with add-on accessories. Unfortunately, they were little more than gimmicks. They included, for example, small plastic shields that were placed on the bonnet to deflect flies from hitting the windscreens, and chains that dangled from the back which were supposed to discharge static electricity thought to cause travel sickness.

Regular maintenance, besides

The joys of motoring: the well-stocked parts department at Jackson's Garage, where motorists could buy those little extras to add to their cars, as well as essential items to keep them on the road.

Newspaper advertisements from the *Surrey Times* of the 1950s for Puttocks Garage and Coombs Service Station.

simply checking the level of oil and water, included the greasing of the steering column every thousand miles or so. Valves had to be decarbonised and ground down every 10,000 miles.

By this time, road tax had been standardised at £12 10s, and was no longer calculated according to engine size. The driving licence was renewable every year for five shillings.

When a driver managed to save up for a new car, it was often bought without accessories such as hub caps or a radio. These had to be saved up for and were perhaps bought as Christmas or birthday presents.

The new Elizabethans

King George VI's death in February 1952 came as a great shock to people all around the world.

However, in the UK, after the official period of court mourning, morale was boosted with the impending coronation of the young Princess Elizabeth. The date was fixed, 2 June 1953, and the countdown had begun.

There was a feeling of well-being and excitement and the sense that Britain was on the verge of a new age. A new Elizabethan age, from which would spring wonders similar to those of the first Elizabethan age. An age of Drake and Shakespeare.

Schoolchildren in Guildford were taught the words to *Land Of Hope And Glory* in readiness for a spectacular event in Stoke Park.

Commemorative items were issued, including, here in Guildford, a mug with both a picture of the new queen and the coat of arms of the borough.

There were other treats too. Guildford women who had reached the age of 60 years, on the presentation of their pension books, received a pound of tea! Likewise, men who were widowed, or bachelors over the age of 65, could also apply.

Coronation Day finally arrived, but it proved more like a winter's day – the weather was dismally wet. 'It rained on her parade' was one comment. In fact, it was the coldest June day for more than 12 years.

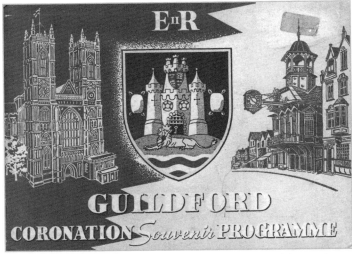

Souvenir programme of the events in Guildford to celebrate the coronation of Queen Elizabeth II on 2 June 1953.

As part of the celebrations in Guildford, the preceding evening had witnessed a civic service conducted on the steps of Holy Trinity Cathedral Church, led by the Very Revd Walter Boulton, Provost of Guildford. The Queen's Regiment, the Women's Royal Army Corp and the Home Guard represented the armed forces. Members of most of the voluntary services within the borough were also present. The service marked the start of an all-night vigil in the church for the new queen, which was followed by holy communion at 7.45am.

The great day itself was announced in the traditional way with a *feu de joie* (fire of joy) – the setting off of small canons in the Castle Grounds. This was followed at 8.30am by the ringing of the bells of Holy Trinity Cathedral Church.

Many Guildfordians then switched on their wireless sets to listen to the events in London. Only a fraction of households owned a television set at the time. So parties were arranged for less fortunate neighbours to drop in to those who had a TV and watch the spectacle of the Coronation inside Westminster Abbey being broadcast live for the first time.

Those post-war TVs were very primitive. Screens were only nine or 12 inches wide. They came with just an on/off switch and a brightness control. The BBC was the only broadcaster.

Those who were lucky enough to watch the coronation live on TV may well have had a set like this one, advertised by Multi-Broadcast.

On the Saturday before there had been a Coronation street party in Vernon Way, Westborough, where more than 100 children enjoyed sports and fancy dress events. There were decorations of red, white and blue, and an iced cake decorated with Union Jack flags.

Coronation ballpens with the inscription 'Waltham Avenue' were presented to 90 children from that area of Stoughton. Likewise, children in Onslow Village were given commemorative pencils. Waltham Avenue itself held a party with the added attraction of a number of hanging baskets filled with paper flowers.

Two hundred children in Charlotteville enjoyed a party with special guests the Mayor and Mayoress. These children also received pens coloured red, white and blue.

Old-time entertainment by a Mr Tidbury was the order of the day for children at Gravetts Lane, Worplesdon, who were treated to a party in the canteen of the nearby Harper's works. In Wood Street, on the Wednesday, there was supposed to have been a picnic tea on the green, but the bad weather put paid to that. Instead Mr Fisher, of Rightene Nursery, came to the rescue and cleared his largest greenhouse of some 4,000 potted plants so that more than 300 children could enjoy their party.

The main event of Chilworth's celebrations was a mammoth carnival procession that wended its way through the village during the afternoon of Coronation day. There was a carnival parade at Albury too, and medals, brooches and mugs were handed out to all children under the age of 15.

West Clandon's Coronation committee and a number of its senior citizens entertained children in the village hall. There was a fancy-dress competition at the British Legion hall, as well as races for the youngsters. There were sports events for adults and children alike on the common at Shalford.

The only call for Guildford Fire Brigade on Coronation day was to a chimney fire at 27 Mangles Road in Bellfields.

CHAPTER TWO

GROWING UP

Schooldays

Schools before the watershed 1944 Education Act were still quite elementary, with their roots deeply set in the Victorian era. The slogan 'spare the cane and spoil the child', was popular; although girls seemed to be exempt from this.

Much attention was given to learning by rote. The only mechanical aid was the abacus.

Until World War Two, there was little provision for nursery education for children of ordinary working people in Guildford.

However, once the war had begun, and with many mothers employed in work of national importance, Guildford opened a number of nursery centres for children aged between two and five years.

The Guildford Education Committee began to discuss the idea at the end of 1940. The *Surrey Advertiser* of 3 May 1941 reported Home Secretary Herbert Morrison's visit to Guildford, during which he opened Britain's first prefabricated nursery centre at Westborough. It wrote: 'He [Morrison] praised the beauty, utility and economy of the new centre.'

It was funded by generous individuals including Lady Allen of Hurtwood, donations from 'friends' in the USA and the Guildford Education Committee.

On 5 July 1941, the *Surrey Advertiser* noted that there were now five nursery centres in Guildford, attended to full capacity by about 180 children. A second prefabricated centre had opened in Stoughton and others had been opened at Rectory Place, St Nicolas Hall, and at Merrow. However, there was a waiting list for places and a proposal was put forward to buy a Gyproc prefabricated building to extend the accommodation at Westborough School, for the use of evacuated children.

'Guildford will have provision for 420 children in wartime nurseries when the present programme is completed,' reported the *Surrey Advertiser* on 28 August 1943. It noted that plans for the Shepherd's Hill Nursery in Stoughton Recreation Ground, off Worplesdon Road, had been approved.

Building work was to start almost immediately, and when completed it would accommodate 70 children up to five years of age and 18 babies under two years. The prefabricated building was to be used from 7.30am to 7.30pm each day and would be centrally heated.

In June 1945, Councillor Mrs G. Croke told members of the Guildford branch of the Nursery

Pupils from St John's School in Farnham Road in about 1947–48. Back row, from left: Anne Davage, Eric Groves, Valerie Gibbs, Ray Barnes, Maureen Pentecost, Sheila Rose, John Crowther, Christine Madder. Middle row: Janet Marshall, Judith Ward, David Baxell, Georgina Wichman, Mr Burston, Anne Ferguson, Paul Matthews, Jean Baxter, Michael Broburg. Front row: Pat Walters, Michael Webster, Janet Rose, Audrey Humphries, Margaret Davis, Michael Rogers.

On the playing field at Bellfields School in the late 1930s.

Girls from Stoughton Junior School pictured in the late 1930s.

School Association that parents were asking for the existing hutment nursery schools to be retained after the war.

The Shepherd's Hill Nursery was particularly popular and children who went there would move on to Stoughton Infant and Junior School in Stoughton Road and then usually to Northmead Boys' or Girls' Schools in Grange Road. If a pupil passed their 11-plus exam, a place at a grammar school was offered.

An alternative to Northmead Boys' School was the Central School in Harvey Road. This was something like a second-grade grammar school. Subjects such as woodwork, instead of the classics, were taught. One of its headmasters was Mr C.E. Nicklin, a former borough councillor and Mayor. His wife taught English at the school.

The 11-plus exam, at such a tender age, could mark a child for life as either a manual or a clerical worker. Taken in the final year of primary or prep school, it consisted of three papers: a mental arithmetic test, an essay question on a general subject, and a general solving paper, assessing ability to apply logic to simple problems and to test general knowledge.

Schooling in Guildford during the war proved to be a difficult time. Stoughton Junior School, next to Stoughton Barracks, for example, was taken over for a time by the army, which needed extra space following the influx of men posted there for military training. Pupils were forced to have lessons in private houses.

Many schools had to accommodate extra pupils who had been evacuated to Guildford. Desks had to be shared, and, as a result, children did not receive the full number of hours of education that they should have had. Lessons could also be interrupted by the sounding of the air-raid siren, followed by the teachers leading their pupils to the school's shelters.

A survey of pupils in Guildford on 5 October 1943 showed that 2,516 children out of 4,411 took their midday meal at school. A canteen was opened at Sandfield School on 1 November 1944, relieving the pressure on the canteen at nearby Stoke School. The kitchen for it was installed at 23 Stoke Road, a house owned by the borough.

Stoke School not only took pupils from the local catchment area, but also some children from the Southern Railway's orphanage. The school was noted for its drama productions and these were well attended by the public.

As in all schools at the time, corporal punishment was freely administered for those misbehaving. A rap on the head with the teacher's knuckles was commonplace, as was, of course, the cane. Swearing was punished by pupils being made to wash their mouths out with soap!

The nearby Sandfield Boys' School once had five masters plus the headmaster, Mr Westmore, who were all sterling characters. Most of them had served in the army during World War One and had endured some very hard times. The deputy head (later to become headmaster) was John Gardiner, the subject of a separate article in this book.

With a baton, Mr Ramsay conducted the pupils' singing at morning assembly. Not only did he announce the number of each hymn, but would call out the number of beats to the bar for the tune to be sung to. At the piano was a Mr Mason, a cheerful character, always ready with a merry quip.

'Frosty' Hoare had been another member of Kitchener's Army, and would occasionally regale his pupils with reminiscences of the Western Front. 'Nobby' Clarke was a bluff, straightforward north country man, with an accent to match. He was a plain speaking, no nonsense type, who wore a large peaked cap.

A student teacher who came to Sandfield Boys' School was Ronald Smoothey. He had been a pupil at the Royal Grammar School, and later went on to be an art master there. He taught at the Royal Grammar School for many years

Pupils from Westborough School taking part in an inter-school singing competition held at Guildford Technical College. They are being conducted by Miss Lynch.

and became well known in Guildford's art world, both for his skill as a painter and for his ability to organise art exhibitions.

The alternative route to state schooling was through the private education system. Beginning with kindergarten, a child would progress from preparatory school to possible entry into a public school. The system of progression was much the same then as it is today, with the Common Entrance exam taken.

St Nicolas' School choir in full voice in 1957.

One such Guildford kindergarten was St Joan's in Aldershot Road. During the 1940s, each day began with a short prayer followed by the headmistress, Miss Vera, playing the hymn *All Things Bright And Beautiful* on her violin. A former pupil remembers that one child, whose parents had managed to flee from Nazi Germany, always arrived after the prayer session. Her parents believed that, because of the privations they had suffered, there could be no God.

The school met in an ordinary three-bedroom house and consisted of two classrooms divided by a partition which was closed after school assembly. The younger children were occupied by threading beads on to a piece of wire. The older group would make up bundles of 10 little sticks which would then be secured by a rubber band.

The morning always finished with a David and Goliath-type of story. Most of the children walked to school, even those whose parents had cars. This was not from choice but because of the shortage of petrol for private use.

When old enough, Guildford children in private education would perhaps go on to St John's, also known as Guildford Borough Preparatory School.

Times tables would be recited in unison by the whole class. Pre-reading was practised by phonetic sounds of the

Boys from Northmead School in Grange Road in 1953. The headmaster, Mr 'Pecker' Howells, is seated sixth from the left in the front row.

alphabet. Letters were then copied from the blackboard and made up into words. Considerable excitement followed when pupils were able to try joined-up writing.

Much attention was given to the style of handwriting and not the subject matter. Neat handwriting was likely to lead to better job prospects in later life. The up stroke of the pen had to be slight, while the down stroke had to be firm. The words had to slope forwards and not lean backwards. The steel ink pens would write up to about six words before they had to be dipped back into the ink well. However, without warning an ink blot would appear on the page.

If the index finger was not held straight, the position was know as the 'pig's knuckle'. Giving a child a slap or a 'boxed ear' was thought to do the trick.

Left-handed children were often forced to write with their right hands, as clerical jobs were not always given to those who had what was then regarded as a dreadful malady.

John Gardiner

'When your mother and father desert you, the Lord will take you up.' A young pupil-teacher was told these words before a train took him away from his parental home in Wales, after an apparent family problem. He later became one of the most respected teachers and lay readers in Guildford. His name was John Gardiner.

Pupils listen attentively to John Gardiner at his York School for Boys.

The time of his life-changing train journey was at about the turn of the 20th century when school discipline was never questioned. In later years his cane literally made a mark on many Guildford schoolboys.

John Gardiner started as a pupil-teacher at the age of 13 at Haverfordwest in Pembrokeshire, earning about a shilling a week.

In 1906, he became an assistant master at Abinger School in Surrey, where his wages rose to £2 a week. He then came to Guildford to teach at Charlotteville School before moving on to Sandfield School where, in 1939, he became headmaster.

However, when retirement beckoned, John Gardiner had no wish to end his teaching career. At the age of 69 he opened his own one-man school in a room in the hall of the Chertsey Street Baptist Church. It was called the York School for Boys and he specialised in coaching pupils who had failed their 11-plus exams, getting them ready to resit them the following year. Fees ranged from £6 to £8 per term.

Over the years he learned his profession so well that he was able to teach almost any subject. He was a stickler for neat and tidy handwriting and discipline was his watchword. Boxed ears or a thorough good shaking were common for any child thought to be slacking.

John Gardiner bought his canes from Fogwills the seed merchants in Friary Street. The cane was applied to pupils when the timing seemed appropriate. The first two applications would be received across the top of the fingers of each hand. If a third caning was required, this would be six strokes across the buttocks with the culprit stretched over the desk. Sometimes the corporal punishment was administered so harshly that the cane literally broke in two, with one end spinning up towards the very high ceiling of the classroom.

Brutal by today's standards? Perhaps, but it brought results. Did parents complain? Sometimes, but they were then asked to remove their boy from Gardiner's private school.

John Gardiner taught at Albury School, Charlotteville School, became headmaster at Sandfield School, and ran his own one-man school, York School for Boys, in Chertsey Street.

However, there was an incident at Sandfield School where a pupil's quick reactions caught John Gardiner off-guard, and for once the tables were turned.

The pupil, who was very tall for his age, at least 6ft, and a known troublemaker, was called to the front of the class for punishment. On the descent of the cane to the miscreant's hand, he grasped the cane and wrenched it from John Gardiner's hand and then set about him with it.

News of this went around the school like wildfire, especially as the two classes either side of John Gardiner's classroom were able to watch what was going on through the glass windows of the separating screens.

John Gardiner taught his own son Peter, and although he never had the cane from his father, he once suffered the indignity of being dragged out in front of his classmates by his father and shaken across the room by the scruff of his neck.

It was the custom at Sandfield that when boys were

leaving the school they would obtain the signatures of their masters in an autograph book, which was usually accompanied by some quotation by each teacher. John Gardiner was skilled at calligraphy, and, when asked for a signature, he would take the autograph book home with him.

It would be returned with a page filled with a biblical quotation or other thought-provoking verse copied out in beautiful handwriting, the capital letters being illuminated in red ink.

This painstaking work must have taken time to produce in just one book, let alone in the number of books submitted for similar signature.

While at Sandfield School, John Gardiner was one of a remarkable team of masters who achieved a steady flow of scholarship entrants to the Royal Grammar School. With elementary school class sizes of 40 boys, that was no mean achievement.

Still teaching at the age of 81, John Gardiner was the subject of a story in the *Daily Express* after he had been anonymously singled out in a Ministry of Education report. The report stated: 'After surveying this virtuoso performance for two days, the inspectors concluded that as long as the proprietor of this school remains as capable and versatile as he still is, the very thorough and valuable work will continue to be done.'

The newspaper found out who he was and sent reporter Rosalie MacRae to Guildford to interview him. John Gardiner appears to have taken this degree of fame in his later years in his stride. The reporter wrote: 'The old and venerable head locked away his cane yesterday and wiped clean the three blackboards.

'Then he adjusted his hearing aid and announced to the assembled boys: 'I am Sir Oracle. When I open my mouth, let no dog bark. This afternoon we adjourn to the cricket field without further expostulations!'

'The 42 boys of York School cheered, and said to one another: "Johnnie is in a good mood today."

'Mr Gardiner snorts with fury at any comparison with Mr Chips.

'Yesterday, in the school's single ink-stained classroom, the boys came up one by one to Mr Gardiner's rostrum to say: "Excuse me, sir. My father is asking if you are the head master everybody is asking about."

'Smile after smile broke over Mr Gardiner's pippin-brown face as he confessed that indeed he was the one.

'Over at the school's cricket pitch in Stoke Park, Mr Gardiner – grey-haired, booming voice, looking spruce and sixtyish in a green tweed suit – gave the boys some tips on fast bowling.

'Then he relaxed in the grass and talked a little about his life.'

The reporter wrote that John Gardiner told her that his maxim had been to teach pupils to be good first and clever afterwards, and to honour their parents – 'as it says in the Bible'. He said that most of all he deplored lateness and dishonesty – 'and that is when the cane comes out'.

One of his blue-blazered pupils, John Hollands, 16, told the reporter: 'He's a wonderful head. We have more fun in this school than anywhere else I know. Not that he's an easy old man, or anything like that. He's a stern disciplinarian.'

Eleven-year-old Nigel Warne (who, the *Daily Express* claimed, had been caned for talking the day before) said: 'He uses the cane at least twice a day, and when he's not doing that he's making you write lines like "punctually is the politeness of princes".'

'All my friends wish they were at this school, but there is a waiting list already.'

Toys and games

Guildford's most popular toy shop used to be the Dolls Hospital in Swan Lane. It did indeed offer a repair service for dolls, as families became so attached to their children's dolls that they couldn't bear to throw one away if it became broken.

For boys, the shop sold Dinky toys. These were very popular as they had rubber tyres which made them into competition cars. Boys would hold contests to see which car rolled the furthest. Small cups, modelled from the silver paper that came in cigarette packets, were presented as prizes.

'Meccano' was popular and resistant to hard play. It was handed down from one child in a family to

'Can she be repaired?' Sheila Brown (now Shelia Atkinson) back in the 1940s with a broken doll at the Dolls Hospital in Swan Lane.

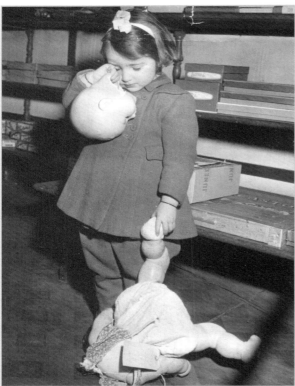

another. Also popular were toy soldiers made of lead. They would often lose their heads, but with the aid of a matchstick, could be reattached to the body. Lead was toxic, so children were warned not to put them in their mouths.

Many wartime toys were made from cardboard and were therefore quite fragile. During those difficult financial days, parents had an unlikely ally. It was called the Squander Bug. It was a cartoon figure with a bulbous body on which was a small head. The creature had wire-like arms and legs, and its body area was covered in swastikas. Parents who wasted money buying toys indiscriminately would in turn aid the Squander Bug in his task to win the war for the Nazis.

Guildford's main sports shop was S.R. Jeffery & Son Ltd, in the High Street. Later, County Sports in Epsom Road, opposite the Odeon cinema, opened. But for many children of working families, being bought new sports equipment was unheard of.

Cricket bats were fashioned from wooden boxes and wickets chalked on wooden fences. Threadbare tennis balls would be used again and again. These would double up as footballs. Real leather footballs existed, but if without a rubber bladder, as rubber was scarce, would be stuffed with newspaper. Girls played their own games separately from the boys. Skipping was a popular pastime. This was enjoyed solo or in a group with the chanting to some rhythmic verse such as 'Nebucanezer King of the Jews, sold his wife for a pair of shoes'. Girls also played housekeeping games, pretending to cook and so on.

Spinning tops were popular, whipped with a piece of cord to keep them rotating; while wooden hoops would be chased along and struck with a stick to keep them going.

Those boys with a bicycle would place pieces of cardboard in the brake assembly to produce the sound of a motor. However, this tended to loosen the spokes. Bikes would become imaginary buses with bus-stop names chalked in the road. Fights with pea shooters versus water-pistols were great fun, as were shoot-outs with potato-guns.

Local newspaper advertisements from the 1950s for Pimms and the Dolls Hospital (below).

The choir of St Francis' Church, Beckingham Road, Westborough, with the Revd Hedley Shearing and other members of the congregation.

St Francis' Church and its choirboys

Churches encouraged young people to sing regularly in their choirs and one of those was St Francis' in Westborough, where Dorothy Parsons was the choirmistress.

She drove back and forth to the church in a 1935 Morris 12 saloon car and was very much of the old school of church music.

She ruled the choir with a rod of iron and devised a system whereby the efficiency of the choir was judged by the ability of a choirboy to sing a psalm solo.

Choirboys who could not get this right would lose as much as sixpence a month from their pay of two shillings.

Singing at a wedding, however, did have its compensations, as another two shillings and sixpence could be earned.

Local photographer Norman Button, who took this picture outside St Francis' Church, is remembered as saying to those gathered: 'The sun is very cruel today.' Deep shadows can clearly be seen and some of the faces have a strained look.

The year was 1949 and the vicar was the Revd Hedley Shearing. He had not long returned from the army in which he served as a chaplain. He was a kindly man who lived with his mother.

The reverend used a whole sermon once to justify the building of a new vicarage next door to the church in Beckingham Road. He said that people would, without doubt, see it as a palace, but the parish must provide adequate accommodation if the church was to attract a vicar with a family. The house in Weston Road in which he lived at that time was woefully inadequate as a vicarage.

St Francis' Church ran a popular youth club on Friday evenings at Foxburrows Hall in Westborough. Square dancing was very popular among the various activities on offer. It really was all the rage, spurred on by popular Westerns being shown at the cinema. A popular song at the time, constantly played on the club's 78rpm gramophone, was *For Every Drop Of Rain That Falls A Flower Grows*. The ever-resourceful Revd Shearing even worked this into one of his sermons, with great effect.

Some of those pictured are, back row: far left, Derek Pollard, who became well known in the local Scout movement; second from the left, David Paddock from Weston Road; fourth from the left, Bernard Parke; sixth from the left, David Fry, the churchwarden's son; third from the right, Richard Holt, from Grantley Gardens; extreme right, Gerald Tribe.

Middle row: second from the left, Mrs Cook; fifth from the left, Mr Wilkin, the headmaster of Bellfields School; third from the right, Mrs Matthews; second from the right, Mrs Nash; far right, Mrs Honeyman.

Front row: from the left: Joan Lloyd; Valerie Wasp, daughter of Major Wasp of the Queen's Regiment; organist and choirmistress Dorothy Parsons; Deaconess Crathorn; the Revd Hedley Shearing; Deaconess Constance Hankin; the churchwarden, Leslie Fry. Far right is Maureen Tilson. She could give a very good presentation of *Oh For The Wings Of A Dove*.

At the time, the photographer Norman Button had not long set up in business at 2 Aldershot Road. His unmarried sister ran a sweet shop and stationers from the same premises.

Youth clubs and other pastimes

The comedian Tony Hancock once referred to the Young Conservatives (YCs) as a 'marriage bureau'. Although this was supposed to be a joke, there was a lot of truth in his comment.

Together with the the Young Farmers, sports clubs and youth clubs, this was the best way to meet members of the opposite sex, which in many cases did indeed lead to marriage.

Politics was a long way down the agenda for the YCs. In Guildford, during the 1950s, meetings usually took place on Thursday evenings with about 80 to 90 members attending.

A wide range of activities were on offer. In fact, the Guildford YCs crewed a rowing four that competed at most of the main Thames regattas.

There was a music group run by a young *Surrey Advertiser* reporter, Bob Benjafield. However, social events were the most popular. A favourite meeting place and watering hole was the coffee bar in the town centre known as Boxers. It was run with a rod of iron by a New Yorker, Mrs Galloway.

Frothy coffee, in perspex cups and saucers, was ninepence a cup. Public houses were largely no-go areas and clubbing was only heard of when talking about cave men! Drugs were to be a problem for the next generation.

Young people would meet in Boxers on a Saturday evening and discuss which dance or event to go to that night. The Young Conservatives also ran very popular monthly dances at the Stoke Hotel, which were enjoyed by young people of all political leanings. These were the days of beauty contests and the YCs ran one each year. They were judged by the then Guildford MP, Dick Nugent, later Lord Nugent. He was often supported by Jack Weatherill, association chairman, who later became Speaker of the House of Commons.

The occasional jazz concert would be on the menu at the nearby Dorking Halls, at which top names such as Chris Barber and Monty Sunshine would play. The highlight of the year was the annual South East meeting, held over a weekend at Eastbourne. More than 1,000 YC members would

Four members of the Guildford Rowing Club, all of whom were also Young Conservatives.

Stoke Youth Club's ninth birthday party on 19 March 1949.

Members of Stoke Youth Club paint the scenery for their pantomime *Ali Baba and the Forty Thieves*. It was produced and directed by John Chasty and was performed at Stoke School in Markenfield Road.

Members of Bellfields Youth Club's netball team.

gather there. The event attracted top Tory party MPs such as Ted Heath and Enoch Powell. However, not all members remained loyal to the Conservative Party; in fact one former Guildford YC member is now a Liberal Peer.

The Liberals tried to emulate the YCs by holding a ball with a Spanish cabaret at the Plaza ballroom in Onslow Street, now Harper's nightclub.

A young Roman Catholic group formed a social club called the Amigo, which met in rooms above the old fire station in North Street. Mass was celebrated at St Joseph's Church on Sunday mornings, and

Girls from Onslow Youth Club dressed up for a drama production in the 1940s.

in the summer months they'd then go off on trips to places such as the Witterings on the West Sussex coast.

Youth clubs were extremely popular and well provided for in Guildford in the late 1940s and 1950s. These included the Onslow, Bellfields, Stoke, Westborough and Charlotteville clubs. Each club had an adult leader and a committee made up of its members. Some clubs had extra adult helpers. These were often people who had become too old to be members, but did not want to leave!

The Stoke club met three evenings a week at Stoke School in Markenfield Road. On average, it had about 80 members, whose ages ranged from 15 to 23 years. Activities included dancing lessons on Monday evenings, led by Doris and Peter Shepherd. Tuesday was a social evening, followed on Friday with ballet lessons for the girls, while the boys played games such as table tennis.

The Onslow club, which met at Onslow School, also offered dancing lessons. These were given by a Phyllis Weaver and her sister. There were also opportunities for boys to learn skills such as woodwork, plus there were gym nights.

Drama featured strongly at the youth clubs too. Each year, the Stoke club staged popular pantomimes at Stoke School that ran for about three nights, which helped to raise funds for the

Band practice for members of Stoke Youth Club.

Stoke Youth Club's 1954 production – *Sinbad the Sailor.*

club. The enterprising young people also raised money for their costumes by holding jumble sales. Members either acted, produced or worked backstage to ensure the productions were a success.

The Guildford Youth Committee included members from the various youth clubs and similar organisations. It also organised events and drama productions with participation from all the local clubs. There was, of course, a good deal of friendly rivalry between the various clubs.

There was an annual display of physical recreation, usually held at Guildford Technical College. The MC was Tom Pope – Guildford's youth and physical training officer.

Drama productions by the Guildford Youth Council Repertory Company included a show called *By The Wey*, which ran for two nights in October 1949, at the technical college's hall. A production of *A Midsummer Night's Dream* was staged on the lawn of Stoke Park Mansion.

Guildford youth clubs also came to the rescue of the borough council when it had a shortage of labour to cut the grass in Stoke and The Mount cemeteries.

Weekend camping at the Chantries was another popular pastime. These camps took place at times such as Easter and Whitsun. Members from Guildford's various youth clubs got together along with clubs from further afield such as Epsom and London.

Members of the 9th Guildford Scout Troop in the late 1940s.

There were also clubs aimed at those who were in their twenties. By the end of the 1940s, Guildford's Over 18s Club was going strong. It first met at the Orphanage Hall in Guildford Park, until members bought a redundant army hut and re-erected it on a strip of land between the River Wey and the Co-op dairy near the Woodbridge Meadows. The Senior Club was also popular. The town's youth officer, Tom Pope, had instigated it by recruiting some 'age expired' members from the town's youth clubs to run it. It met at a vacant rugby pavilion in Stoke Park. Members met several evenings a week, including weekends, to play table tennis and billiards. There was a small library, a quiet room and a kitchen.

In the summer months there were tennis tournaments, rounders at the Chantries campsite and trips to the seaside. In the winter, members went on rambles, held concerts and raised club funds by activities such as carol singing and scrub clearing on The Mount.

In about 1952, the rugby club asked for its pavilion back, so the Senior Club moved to a hut in the lido car park. A recruitment drive brought in new members and eventually the name was changed to The Lantern Club.

The advent of the swinging Sixties and a change in lifestyle – with more TV, higher wages, more cars and so on, saw to the end of such clubs for young adults. However, some of the former members of the Senior Club and Lantern Club are still in touch and have held occasional reunions.

Guildford Technical College

Thousands of young Guildfordians at some time or other will have had contact with Guildford Technical College, now called Guildford College.

Much of the college was built in the 1930s, although with additions in the 1950s with the help of the college's own building department. Further buildings on the campus have been added in recent years. Its predecessor was in Park Street, which later became the Education Office.

Educational opportunities in the 1950s were very much at a premium. This was a last chance for the failed candidates of the earlier selection exams to redeem themselves and to take their O-levels and then A-levels. The one-year O-level course was free, but an entrance examination had to be taken as education was then regarded as a burden on the rate-payer. Students aimed to pass at least five O-levels.

They were joined by many of the private education pupils from Cranleigh, Tormead and other local fee-paying schools, whose parents no doubt decided that the fees were becoming a burden on them.

Some of these young people found the sudden freedom too much and tended to skip lectures, with devastating results.

This section of the technical college was known as the Commerce Department. It came under the control of a small and fiery Scot by the name of Mr McGinnis.

The building also housed the Junior Technical School, on the lower floor, and the Girls' Day Commercial School, on the upper floor. The latter was governed by the headmistress, Miss Gillespie, whose team taught shorthand and typing to young women.

The Guildford School of Art enhanced the building on the west side with its distinctive columns. It later transferred to Farnham.

Some of those who went to the technical college were day-release students, who were in employment as apprentices. Few students from the tech went on to university.

At seven in the evening an army of people, both young and old, would appear after a hard day's work to further hone their skills and so improve their lot in life. Perhaps the largest contingent was that of the banks, under the guidance of Reg Saunders. It was at Guildford tech that many struggling young bank clerks strived to gain their Associate of Chartered Institute of Banking Certificates, which in some cases led to a board appointment as a manager.

Tradespeople also made up a motley crowd. The butcher from Stoughton, Frank Sparrow, often cursed the fact that he had to struggle up the flights of steps with a side of beef to reach his teaching

The 1954 intake of the commerce department at Guildford Technical College. The then principal of the technical college, Dr Topping, is seated in the front of the picture, while the head of the commerce department is seated on his right-hand side. Mr Newmark, the linguist, is pictured second from the left. The other front-row teaching staff include: Mr Burnett (history), Mr Durrant (mathematics), Miss Coward (English literature) and Miss Stirrup (English language).

area on the top floor. His classes taught the butcher boys how to cut out the Sunday joint to the customer's liking. Charlie and Bill Pollard, of Pollard Bros, were involved with teaching the plumbing apprentices.

It was in 1954 that Guildford experienced its first 'rag day' in the town centre, courtesy of students from the tech. The idea was to collect money for charity; the most popular way was to steal items that would then be returned for a small contribution. A model figure of a dog, with the unique name K9, was taken from outside a shop in Park Street. The shop sold dog food. The eagle emblem above Barclays Bank was also liberated. The whole affair went rather sour when the police raided the college, closing the main iron gates, incarcerating all within.

The principal of the college in 1954 was Dr Topping. He was succeeded by the colourful character of Dr Stott. He was a man before his time, who relished more adventurous leisure pursuits such as shark fishing. He was also interested in using a crossbow. Once, while giving a talk and demonstration in the main hall with such a weapon, whether with intention or not, he let loose the bolt, which shot out and embedded itself in the woodwork of the balcony. It was one way to empty the hall in an emergency!

An aerial picture postcard view of Guildford Technical College that is believed to date from about the time of World War Two.

Some students had the opportunity to attend the matriculation department that was run by a Mrs Ward. She is remembered as rather eccentric and out of touch with the outside world. She was a kindly person and a good teacher although she cared little for her own appearance.

The department included an assortment of students, such as those who were poor at commercial subjects, plus a sprinkling of ex-servicemen. As a result, debating was lively, and although the curriculum was something of a mystery to many, it was inspiring. For example, a student who was hopeless at maths would probably be entranced by lessons on Pythagoras' theorem!

The social side of the college revolved around the common-room with its three table-tennis tables. Occasionally a gramophone player was brought in. In winter, during lunch breaks, students who had their lessons in the huts sat around the stoves to keep warm.

CHAPTER THREE

PASTIMES AND LEISURE

At the cinema

'Standing at one and ninepence!' This was a familiar cry from the smart commissionaire who would patrol the long cinema queues in Guildford.

'Patrol' was the right word, for he and his companions at all the Guildford cinemas were of a military bearing, often sporting a small waxed moustache. These were popular among senior army NCOs. Indeed, senior NCO's chevrons would often be worn with pride on the sleeves of his uniform. This was then completed with a service-style dress cap placed smartly on a head of close-cropped hair.

The commissionaire's job was to parade up and down the long queues of bedraggled would-be cinema goers to ensure order. It was done with the dignity only known on the parade ground.

Bedraggled? Yes, for it always seemed to rain when queues formed outside cinemas. Especially when a popular picture was being shown. On the commissionaire's command, the hopeful standing-only patrons would break ranks and leave the queue in the hope that at least they might catch the start of the main picture.

Once in the relative comfort of the cinema they would stand orderly at the back and wait for a seat to become vacant. The commissionaire's counterpart within the building was the usherette. Armed with a torch, she would also keep order. However, the back row was a sort of no-go area as this section was noted for its heavy petting.

Seats became vacant during the performance as people would enter and leave the cinema at any time during the show. They might even stay on to see the film over and over again if they had nowhere else to go or nothing to do.

Prices for seats varied according to where they were in the cinema. At the Guildford Odeon, the more expensive seat applicants, which went up to the value of three shillings and sixpence, would form a queue which snaked its way up Jenner Road. The queue for the cheaper seats, which could be as low as ninepence, would wind its way down the upper High Street.

There was confusion when the Atlee government introduced an entertainment tax which put as much as threepence on the price of a seat. In those dreary days of the late 1940s, entertainment was regarded as a luxury and was taxed as such.

Guildford Odeon in Epsom Road with its classic Art Deco façade.

Staff at Guildford Odeon in the 1960s. The manager, Bryan Richardson, is on the far right.

Like all entertainment of that period, smoking was the order of the day. It was quite amazing the designs and shapes that the columns of smoke would make as they curled their way through the projector's beam on their way to the ceiling.

As a whole, the audience was quite controlled. However, a certain Bill Haley changed that when his rock 'n' roll film was imported from the States. The beat had some strange effect on young people, who danced in the aisles during the showing. However, Bill was quite tame by today's standards, which makes the whole issue difficult to explain.

Towards the end of the show there would be some disturbance, as just before the final words in the film were spoken there would be a rush for the door. It was thought the stampede was caused by the urge to catch the last bus home. The more enlightened knew it was to avoid standing to attention during the playing of the National Anthem!

Apparently this dates from the days of World War One when soldiers in uniform were obliged to stand to attention, and the civilian population would stand with them as a sign of support.

Children loved the pictures, mainly because on wet afternoons there was little for them to do.

The Guildford Odeon ran a very popular film show for children on Saturday mornings, for as little

High Street entrance to the Playhouse Cinema and Restaurant in the Playhouse Arcade.

as sixpence. And that was well within the average pocket money range. The programme would include about six different films, including a sing-along, which would be conducted by the cinema manager. The theme song started with the words: 'We come along on Saturday morning, greeting everybody with a smile.'

The problem during the week was that children could only buy tickets for certificate U films. They could view an A film with an adult, but X films were definitely out.

It was quite common to see little groups of children standing outside cinemas showing A films. When an adult approached the ticket desk they would ask a man or woman to take them into the show. Dare parents allow children to do that today?

Advertisement from the *Surrey Times* for the Guildford Cinema when it was about to change its name to the Astor in 1959.

Studios 1 and 2 in 1976. The building opened as the Guildford Cinema in 1923. It had an auditorium wider than the norm with recessed curtained panels on each wall that gave the impression of small boxes in a theatre. For many years there were separate pay boxes, one where tickets could be obtained for the cheaper seats and reached down a covered passageway at the side of the building and another for the middle and back stalls and balcony in the foyer. In 1969, by which time it was called the Astor, it was ripped apart inside to create a 'modern image'. Further alterations took place in 1971, when the two screens were created. However, the picture quality was poor and so was the sound proofing between the two screens. It closed as a cinema in 1988 and has since been a nightclub, but is now closed, awaiting demolition as part of the town centre revamp.

The Guildford Odeon was different from the other cinemas as it had a stage and so it was able to put on live shows. The big bands such as Ted Heath with his vocalist Dickie Valentine and Lita Rosa would frequent it.

Once, before the showing of the film *A Night To Remember*, which starred Kenneth More, an officer who had survived the sinking of the ill-fated *Titanic* gave a short talk.

The Odeon at the top of the High Street has gone, along with its smart commissionaires. However, the organisation does live on. Some of the commissionaires of yesteryear are buried in a plot reserved for the Corps of Commissionaires at nearby Brookwood Cemetery. They certainly were a sight to remember.

Theatres

The cradle of modern-day theatre in Guildford is none other than the former St Nicolas' Parish Hall, tucked away in Millmead, where a young Michael Redgrave took part in productions. Since then the town has seen the Guildford Theatre in North Street come and go, to be replaced by today's Yvonne Arnaud Theatre beside the River Wey. In the 1960s, Sir Michael Redgrave came back to the town to play his part in ensuring that it got built.

St Nicolas' Parish Hall was built in 1885 and has served the town well in many ways over the years. It was once a favourite venue for local dances and was the home of the Pope and Pullinger Old Time Dance Club, with its resident band run by a Miss Stapleton.

Its link with local theatre goes back to 1932 when Claud Powell and Dorothy Owen formed the Guildford Repertory Company at the hall. This amateur company was the proving ground for the actor, writer and playwright Sir Michael Redgrave, who at the time was teaching modern languages at Cranleigh School.

His service to the theatre at large is well known, but in his early days in Guildford perhaps one of

The former St Nicolas' Parish Hall in Buryfields, the cradle of modern-day theatre in Guildford. It is currently the Bellairs Playhouse and used by the GSA conservatoire.

his most popular plays was *The Barretts of Wimpole Street*. During this production he insisted that everything had to be right – even down to the props. One of the younger members of the cast was Ernest Ede, who lived in Church Street. He was commissioned to buy a cigar to be smoked by one of the actors at each performance. He didn't have a lot of spare cash, but was able to buy one locally for ninepence. The other actors looked on bemused as Michael Redgrave approached him after one such performance only to say: 'Don't bother with buying those cigars any more, I have found much better ones.'

Performances at the hall went on into 1941 when it was requisitioned for the war effort. As a consequence, Guildford's serious theatre went into hibernation until the Henderson Brothers, Patrick and Roy, established the Guildford Theatre Repertory Company in 1946. (Roy was better known by his stage name, Roger Winton). They financed it themselves and acquired a lease from the Guildford & District Co-operative Society for the site of the former Borough Hall and assize court.

To mere mortals, the refusal of Surrey County Council to issue a stage play licence would have been the end of the project, but not to the Henderson brothers, who then set up a theatre club as a non profit-making distribution trust.

The costs were covered by box office and members' subscriptions. After barely two months the new club boasted nearly 6,000 members. The Playgoers' Society also played an important part in those days, arranging concerts, play readings, lectures and debates to raise an interest in the theatre.

The new theatre club produced a different play each week, with a popular pantomime each year that ran for three weeks. During the 1950s, a then young Peter Sallis (*Last of The Summer Wine* fame) and a not-so-young Wilfred Bramble (*Steptoe & Son*) helped it to blossom.

The theatre club proved a model for other local towns such as Leatherhead. It did much to lighten those dark post-war days. Patrick Henderson died in 1952, during a downturn of interest in live theatre mainly due to the then new medium of television.

Takings fell, but the theatre club received aid from the Arts Council of Britain, which helped to stem the outward cash flow sufficiently to see the theatre through to a tragic night in 1963, when it burned down.

However, this heralded the opening of the Yvonne Arnaud Theatre in 1965 and in less than two decades Guildfordians were able to see a bevy of rising stars, many of whom went on to become household names, such as Kenneth Williams, Patricia Routledge, Frank Findlay and Edward Woodward.

Planning for the Yvonne Arnaud Theatre took off in November 1961 when a trust was formed and a public appeal launched to raise £220,000 to build the theatre. The borough council stepped in with a £20,000 grant and made available the site near the Town Mill at a peppercorn rent.

The foundations being laid for the Yvonne Arnaud Theatre in the summer of 1963.

Captain Nicholas Kempson RN was appointed appeal organiser in March 1962 and soon voluntary fund-raising committees sprang up within a 30-mile radius of Guildford.

Events to raise cash included theatre performances both locally at the civic hall, Loseley Park, Sutton Place, and in village halls, and also in the West End, some with well-known artists taking part.

Paul Daneman and Anthony Newley opened fund-raising fairs in Guildford, Sir Michael Redgrave gave a Hans Christian Anderson recital locally, and one of the first balls at the newly opened civic hall had the added bonus of special guests singer Alma Cogan and the cast from the then popular TV series *Z Cars*.

Publicity was the name of the game and Sir Michael Redgrave helped to keep the emerging theatre's profile high by turning on the mechanism to drive the first pile in October 1962. By that time £90,000 had been raised. His daughter, Vanessa, unveiled the foundation stone on 18 September

On 23 April 1964, actors Rupert Helpmann, Diane Wynyard, Vivien Leigh and Sir Michael Redgrave performed works of Shakespeare to an invited audience of 280 people at the half-finished Yvonne Arnaud Theatre. The event marked the 400th anniversary of the Bard's birthday. Vivien Leigh described the building as marvellous. The half-hour programme started at noon and the 50 construction workers were given an extended lunch break to keep the site clear.

1963, while at the same time 'signing' her visit by placing the sole of her left foot in a block of wet cement.

A newsletter-brochure issued by the trust towards the end of 1963 had a message from Sir Michael Redgrave on the front cover. He wrote: 'I am eagerly looking forward to the opening in Guildford of this exciting new theatre, one of the best of its kind in the world.'

Actress Susan Hampshire performed the topping out ceremony on the roof of the theatre on 11 November 1964 and in the February of that year The Yvonne Arnaud Theatre Management had been formed. It appointed Laurier Lister as its director and administrator. Another important person who devoted much time and energy to see the theatre built was Alderman A.W. Graham Brown. Nicknamed 'Mr Theatre', he had dreamt of a new theatre for Guildford and it was fitting that he was the chairman of the theatre trust.

The grand opening, on 2 June 1965, was a gala night with a host of stars. The *Guildford Times*

Screen star Dirk Bogarde (right) chats to architect John Brownrigg on the opening night of the Yvonne Arnaud Theatre in 1965.

reported: 'A dazzling first night at the Yvonne Arnaud Theatre on Wednesday drew an audience of many hundreds – to watch the audience. Crowds in Millbrook and the theatre forecourt saw leading personalities of British theatre drive up (some walked from a car park along the road) and many distinguished people from other walks of life.

'Loelia, Duchess of Westminster, arrived with the American Ambassador, Mr David Bruce, and his wife, and the French Ambassador, M. Geoffroy de Courcel, and his wife.

'The Vice-Lieutenant of Surrey, Lord Hamilton of Dalzell, was there, the Mayor and Mayoress of Guildford, Sir Richard and Lady Nugent, and Mr Hugh McLellan, widower of Yvonne Arnaud with Lady Auriol Vaughn (Auriol Malet, godchild of Yvonne Arnaud, and her biographer).

'Another Godchild of Yvonne Arnaud, Dirk Bogarde, was there to speak from the stage the prologue specially written by Christopher Fry (who was in the audience).

'Among the last to reach the theatre were Sir Laurence and Lady Olivier, but earlier there had been a cheer from the crowd for Dame Sybil Thorndike and Sir Lewis Casson. They arrived shortly after Sir Donald and Lady Wolfit.

Crowds line the approach to the Yvonne Arnaud Theatre on its opening night to watch the guests arrive.

'Other well-known faces were those of Miss Florence Desmond, Miss Vanessa Redgrave (who came with her husband Mr Anthony Richardson, and Mr John Osborne, the playwright), Miss Jessie Matthews, Mr Rupert Davies and Miss Susan Hampshire – and, of course, the most familiar face among the pressmen, Mr Bernard Levin.'

Sir Michael directed the opening festival that saw him starring alongside Ingrid Bergman in Turgenev's *A Month In The Country*. The festival also saw him play Samson, in John Milton's *Samson Agonistes*, while Anne Rogers took the lead in Dibdin and Bickerstaff's musical comedy *Lionel And Clarissa*. The inclusion of Bergman on the bill meant that Guildford's new theatre became front-page news everywhere.

The *Surrey Advertiser* printed a special supplement telling the story of theatre in the town from the 16th century to the present time. It described the Yvonne Arnaud as a 'theatre for everyone'. And although there was a notice on the page back stating that £75,000 was still needed to complete the payment for the project, the newspaper was confident that the new venture was on firm foundations and its name was on the lips of every theatre-lover in the country.

The entrance to the Yvonne Arnaud Theatre.

Cycle speedway riders from the Dennisville Rockets in 1951–52. From left: Alan Morsley, David Morsley, Jimmy Worsfold, unknown, Malcolm Habgood, Keith Gates (captain), David Shalard, Jimmy Oldfield, Johnny Smither, Neville (first name unknown), and the team manager Mr J. Elton and his wife.

Cycle speedway

Cycle speedway made its first appearance in 1946 on a London bombsite that had been cleared of rubble. This self-styled sport rapidly took off throughout the UK and it was not long before teenagers in Guildford were tearing around circuits made of cinders and ash on recycled bikes without brakes or mudguards. In the borough of Guildford alone at least seven clubs met regularly and the spectacle provided tremendous family entertainment.

The Guildford Aces met on Station Meadows, now known as Woodbridge Meadows. Perhaps their star rider was John Clayton, who was later to have a career with the motorcycle manufacturer BSA. His father was a great promoter of John's talents and was also a popular figure in the town, working from his base at Clares for Spares, situated in the Rodboro Buildings on the corner of Onslow Street and Bridge Street.

Guildford Greyhounds raced around the York Road chalk quarry, where the multi-storey car park is today. Millmead Monarchs held court on the small river island on which the Yvonne Arnaud Theatre now stands. Guildford Park Panthers lurked on Guildford Park recreation ground. Dray Court occupies this site today.

Westway Bluebirds simply flew around a ground near the Ashenden estate, where the Tesco store now stands, while the Stoughton Stars sparkled at Saffron Platt.

And the Dennisville Rockets went into orbit from their base at the bottom of Stag Hill. The site is now a large roundabout. A notable rider was Keith Gates, later to become a watch repairer who worked for many years with Salisbury's in Swan Lane and who also looked after the famous Guildhall clock.

Originally, the bikes used for cycle speedway were ordinary ones with a just few adjustments. However, with the help of proud fathers, they became more customised. The bikes were often ridden to the tracks where the meeting was to be held. Once there, their single back brakes would be removed. It was not permitted to use brakes during a race. The riders looked smart in their bright club tabards as they lined up for the start of each race.

Eventually, a cycle manufacturer marketed a purpose-built bike which was sold by Pascalls from its shop at the junction of Woodbridge Road and North Street. The bike was expensive for the average teenager, retailing at £12. That was almost twice a man's weekly wage in those days.

However, other cycle shops, such as Jackson's on Portsmouth Road, run by a Mr Mitchell, and Weston & Phillips on Woodbridge Road, opposite what was the electricity works, soon took up the challenge and provided a service for this fledgling sport.

Guildford gained some national prestige when a rather youthful Brian Johnson, later to become perhaps the most popular cricket commentator of all time, came with a BBC outside broadcast team to the official opening of the Guildford Aces' new track at Station Meadows.

Stoughton Stars (dark tabards) in action against Godalming Bulldogs.

He had a large microphone attached to him as he gave a live broadcast commentary while riding in a race!

By 1953, the heyday of cycle speedway and the 'skid-kids' who competed so fiercely was over. Boys who had taken part were now growing up and going off to do their National Service. Once they had returned there was no thrill in bikes you had to pedal – motorised machines were much more fun.

Skiffle into rock 'n' roll

For many years Guildford has enjoyed a popular live music scene. Young people had followed dance bands around local venues, such as drill halls and village halls. But as a new generation of youngsters came along other forms of music became the 'in' thing to dance and listen to.

Skiffle enjoyed a brief spell of popularity in the 1950s, and Guildford produced a few of these bands with their home-spun instruments. Youngsters raided their mother's kitchen and father's shed for suitable items that could be adapted as musical instruments.

The wash board, used in the kitchen sink to clean clothing by rubbing against its ribbed surface to remove stains and dirt, was one such implement that was used. Played with sewing thimbles on the musician's fingers, a rhythm could then be drummed out by running them over the ridges on the board.

A double bass-type instrument was made from an old tea chest to which a broom handle was attached, together with a length of string. The tin foil lining of the tea chest helped with the resonance of the thing. A guitar player and singer would be added, and such popular songs as Lonnie Donegan's *Rock Island Line* were played.

The Doolahats were one local skiffle band that got together in about 1957, with Claude Wilkins on guitar and vocals, Mick Cranham on tea-chest bass, Chris Winters on guitar and Chris Arkle on the washboard. In 1958, the line-up changed with Johnny Kelly joining on lead guitar, Chris Arkle switching to snare drum,

Skiffle band the Doolahats. From left: Chris Winters, Chris Arkle, Mick Cranham and Claude Wilkins.

Mick Douglas who, in the late 1950s and early 60s, played in a number of local bands including Johnny Kelly's Rocking Crescendos and the Tropics. He currently fronts popular rock 'n' roll band Razzle Dazzle.

The Tropics pictured in St Francis' Church Hall in Weston Road, in about 1957–58. From left: Roger Fletcher, Chris Crinnel, Owen Window, Jack Thornber and Mick Douglas. Out of view on piano is Bruce Clark.

Les Owen playing bass, Micky Lampard on guitar and Claude Wilkins continuing as front man on vocals and guitar. Later that year Stan Newman came in on washboard.

But rock 'n' roll was about to be unleashed on the world and skiffle didn't really stand a chance. With a little bit more money in their pockets, young people began to afford electric guitars, drum kits and the necessary amplification to put a band on the road – albeit around the local church halls, playing cover versions of the latest hits. Some of the skiffle musicians changed direction and became rock 'n' rollers.

Johnny Kelly had previously had his own skiffle group and, later, he and Claude formed Johnny Kelly's Rocking Crescendos. Musicians who played in this band included Kenny Pate, Micky Fitzpatrick, Micky Woods, Tony Spencer, David Brice and another young guitarist, Mick Douglas.

Mick also played in another Guildford band, the Tropics, with Roger Fletcher, Chris Crinnel, Jack Thornber and Bruce Clark.

Guildford's 'biggest' band of the early 1960s was Phillip Goodhand-Tait and the Stormsville Shakers. They had formed in 1961 when guitarist Ivor Shackleton and bass player Kirk Riddle met up with drummer Paul Demers and vocalist Phillip.

After a couple of years there was a change of line-up that included new drummer, Dick 'Fancy' Forcey, and Steve Howard on tenor sax. An additional sax player, Peter 'Greg' McGregor, then joined. The Shakers' sax section changed yet again with Dave Sherrington and Tony Hurley stepping in.

The band went on to release two LPs plus two singles, *Gonna Put Some Hurt On You* and *No Problem*, the former hitting the lower reaches of the *Melody Maker* charts.

In the early days the band gigged in and around Guildford at venues such as the Plaza and local village halls, while also playing support to bands on tour who were appearing at Guildford Civic Hall. Later, the Shakers would play further afield. It was not uncommon for them to play all-nighter clubs around the country, including the popular Ricky-Tick circuit.

Although the band eventually split, Phillip Goodhand-Tait has become a successful solo musician and songwriter. Kirk Riddle is still a well-known musician based in this area.

In 1963, the Shakers won the Surrey Rock Competition. Their rivals in the final and on the local music scene were the Kossacks. In all, they met each other three times in battle of the bands contests.

The Crescendos pictured at the Plaza in Onslow Street in 1959. Musicians from left: John Moon, Johnny Kelly, David Brice, Laurie Way, Tony Spencer, Les Owen. Sitting is Vince Taylor of the Playboys.

The first occasion was a heat of the Red Cross Rock-Trad Band Contest, when the Kossacks came out on top. A local press report stated: 'When the marks of the three judges were added together the Kossacks were given a points victory, but if audience reaction had been the only factor taken into consideration there is no doubt that the Shakers would have delivered a knock-out blow.'

The report neatly summed up the kind of music each band played: 'Although the Kossacks and the Stormsville Shakers both come under the category of rock groups, their approach and style could not be much farther apart. The Kossacks concentrate on a slick pop sound and score on the versatility side by having a female singer as well as the usual singing guitarists.

'If you called the Shakers slick they would be offended. Theirs is the wild, original rock sound that is gaining favour at the moment through such singers as Chuck Berry and Bo Diddley.'

The leader of the Kossacks was drummer Dave Brice. Previously, he had played guitar with a band called The Rhythm Five and then with Johnny Kelly & The Crescendos. The Kossacks had Caroline Harms on lead vocals, plus Colin Tutton on rhythm guitar, Radley Walker on lead guitar and Dave Shaw on bass. They played plenty of venues and built up a good following but eventually split, never having had a real stab at hitting the big time.

There was a bit of argy bargy when the Shakers and the Kossacks met for the second time in the semi-final of a music contest. It was 1963 and the venue was the Plaza ballroom. The story in the following Wednesday's midweek *Surrey Advertiser* began: 'We would have liked to have shown you on this page a picture of two rock groups shaking hands with one another. But after the results were announced, Dave Brice, leader of the Kossacks, somehow didn't seem interested. Actually his exact words were: "You won't get me posing with any photos with them" – meaning his rivals the Shakers.'

The report added that there were some wild accusations going around that the judges were biased. However, the reporter, believed to have been Mark Ackerman, may have used his journalism skills to flam up the whole episode. Both bands went on to play the final, held at Shalford Park, on Saturday 25 May 1963, but there was to be no luck in store for the Kossacks. When they went on stage to play their set the generator supplying the electricity packed up.

A glance at some of the advertisements in back numbers of the *Surrey Advertiser* in the early 1960s reveals the names and venues where local bands were playing at that time. The Stoke Hotel featured the Clublanders on 6 September 1963, with admission at six shillings. The following week the Neville Jackson Band were playing there. On 21 September 1963, the Plaza held a heat of the £2,000 All Britain Beat Contest. Battling it out were the Stormsville Shakers, the Age Beaters, the Reflections, the Whirlwinds, Unit Six and the Jaguars. Later that year the civic hall was promoting a 'beat nite dance' every Tuesday. Those who appeared included Rob Stone and the Whispers and Ray Pilgrim and the Minutemen.

For a time in the 1960s, the Age Beaters were Guildford's top band, securing residencies at the

Tunsgate Club, which was above Russell & Bromley's shoe shop in the High Street, and the Plaza in Onslow Street. They also had a regular spot supporting Surrey's leading dance band of the time, the Chris Allen Band, at their 'Saturday palais nights' at Guildford Civic Hall.

The Age Beaters included Bert Curtis on drums, Dave Everson on lead guitar and vocals, Peter Cannon on rhythm guitar and Alan Housewell on bass guitar.

The band had a stage act that involved their manager dressing up like Jack the Ripper and being carried in a real coffin into dance halls with the lights dimmed!

They did a photo shoot at St Catherine's Hill one Sunday morning with 'Jack' in full Ripper costume. A local resident saw them and, thinking it was some kind of black magic ritual, called the police.

Singer and guitarist Nigel Enever played skiffle until 1963, when, at the age of 16, he formed a band playing electric instruments that was called the Trolls. They were soon followed by a more substantial group called the Weysiders. This band featured Nigel on lead guitar, Bob Cox on bass, John Enever on drums, Mick Welton on rhythm guitar and Julian Lile on lead vocals.

In 1967, Nigel and his brother John formed another well-known Guildford group, the Switch, with Roger Thackeray on bass, Richard Cayre on organ and Stuart Reffold on vocals. Their sound was influenced by American soul music.

The Phantom Four were yet another Guildford band who were aiming for the big time in the mid-1960s. Their line-up featured Richard Over on rhythm guitar, Alan Butcher on drums, Ian Latimer on bass and vocals and his brother Andy on lead guitar. Indeed, Andy Latimer went on to form the progressive rock band Camel, in which he still plays and which has released more than 30 albums.

The year 1963 year must surely go down in history as one of the greatest for live music in the town, with appearances by none other than the Rolling Stones, who played the civic hall on 15 December, along with Georgie Fame and the Blue Flames, the Graham Bond Quartet, and the Yardbirds, all on the same night!

However, it was the night of 21 June that will be etched in the memory of many, when the Beatles played at the Odeon cinema. The concert was billed as the Jimmy Crawford Package Show. The programme stated that on the bill at Guildford supporting the Beatles would be Lance Fortune, the Hayseeds, the Vampires, Rocking Heart, the Messengers and the Vikings with Michael London. The compére was Vic Sutcliffe. There were two performances at 6.15pm and 8.15pm.

The Beatles arrived at Guildford Odeon in a red convertible Ford Zephyr car, waving to everyone. It was driven along Sydenham Road and past the Rats Castle pub.

The queues went right around the building in the upper High Street and up to Sydenham Road. By all accounts the crowd was very boisterous and noisy. It's said that the Beatles' concert in

The Kossacks pictured at the Plaza in 1961–62. From left: Dave Shaw, Colin Tutton, Caroline Harmes, Radley Walker and David Brice.

The Stormsville Shakers. From left: Ivor Shackleton, Philip Goodhand-Tait and Kirk Riddle.

Guildford seemed to set a precedent in the town for live music. After that it was the norm for people to scream and shout. The security at concert venues soon became much tighter.

Other artists who played the Odeon in the mid-1960s included Billy Fury, Joe Brown, and Shane Fenton – who later changed his name to Alvin Stardust.

The Rolling Stones returned to Guildford in 1964 to play at the Odeon. This was the All Stars '64 tour that featured no fewer than 12 bands and the Stones weren't even top of the bill! That spot was reserved for John Leyton. Also playing were the Le Roys, Billy Boyle, Don Spencer, Billie Davis, Mike Sarne, the Innocents, Jet Harris and Mike Berry.

Ricky-Tick clubs were venues in the home counties, including a Guildford nightclub, that attracted teenagers to hear blues, rock 'n' roll, jazz or rhythm 'n' blues music, often all night and always at least five days a week. They were run by Philip Haywood and John Mansfield from a large mansion, condemned for demolition, in Windsor.

Many American musicians who came to the UK to tour played the Ricky-Tick circuit. They included blues legends such as Howlin' Wolf and Sonny Boy Williamson. Young British bands were used as their backing musicians. A young Stevie Wonder also did the circuit, as did another up and coming British singer-songwriter – Elton John.

The Plaza in Onslow Street became the main Ricky-Tick venue in Guildford. However, Philip Haywood and John Mansfield also booked other local venues and halls as they were establishing their empire. John recalls the night of 9 March 1963 when the pair hired the Wooden Bridge pub for a gig by the Rolling Stones. The pub was full with paying fans and it was just as well that Philip had recruited three new bouncers for the night. Inside, the fans were foot stompin' and hand waving. Girls were perched on other people's shoulders ready to watch the band. Unfortunately, there were a lot of people outside who could not get in. Suddenly, the fire doors were ripped open and more fans started to pour in. The newly recruited bouncers had a struggle to maintain order, which they did with good humour and without resorting to violence.

At the end of the evening, as Philip was paying the bouncers, he expected them to say they were not interested in further work at the Wooden Bridge. However, although their clothes were torn, they were happy – and were looking forward to the following Friday!

By 1966 another live music venue had opened in the Rodboro Buildings in Onslow Street. This was the Harvest

The Switch were formed in 1967. Seen here is the guitarist Nigel Enever and singer Stuart Reffold. Today Stuart is with a band called the Fugatives, along with former Stormsville Shaker, Kirk Riddle.

Moon Club and it also played host to rock, blues and rhythm 'n' blues bands, plus DJs from the world of radio.

Advertisements that appeared in the *Guildford & Godalming Times* of 1966 listed artists that included Rupert Rayles, Four After One, the Deacon Lewis Band, the Blues Syndicate, the Teknecks and the High Brands. The Ricky-Tick boys were also soon using the club under their banner, for one night a week.

By this time the drug culture had hit the UK and Guildford was no exception. It had probably been introduced to the town by outsiders a few years earlier. However, some young people began experimenting with cannabis and pills such as drinamyl – commonly known as 'purple hearts'. The Harvest Moon Club was one venue where illegal drugs were sold by dealers. Young people who were tempted probably knew the risks they were taking if they were caught.

The *Guildford & Godalming Times* of 2 April 1966 reported a case that was heard before local magistrates in which two young men were each fined £25 for the illegal possession of purple hearts following arrest at the Harvest Moon Club. During the hearing, a police inspector said that, in the main, most young people at the club were responsible, decent young people and that the management were 'most anxious to stamp out this sort of thing'.

A kind of link to the 1960s Guildford music venues were the cafes and coffee houses where young people hung out. These included the Continental Cafe in the High Street. It was frequented by Mods, whose scooters were always parked very neatly outside, all facing the same way up the High Street. Boxers, also in the High Street, was another cafe and in Chertsey Street there was a coffee bar called the Bamboo.

The Bamboo had a bit of a bad reputation, although its owner, a Mr Norris, ran it like a headmaster, keeping order at all times. No alcohol was sold on the premises; anyone entering drunk was thrown out, even barred, and drug-taking was unheard of. The place was closed by 9.30pm weekdays and 10.30pm at weekends.

A flight of uncarpeted, rickety stairs led from street level to the coffee bar. At the top was a mirror where girls back-combed and lacquered their hair into bush-like hair styles and applied lashings of mascara, white eye-shadow and pale pink lipstick.

Those who gathered there drank frothy coffee, bottles of Coca-Cola, glasses of fresh orange juice from a container where a plastic orange bobbed, or ice-cold milk. There were pin tables and loud music throbbed from the jukebox. Everyone jived and twisted on the concrete floor, the girls wearing holes into the soles of their stiletto-heeled shoes.

CHAPTER FOUR

LOCAL BUSINESSES

Drummond Bros

Brothers Frank and Arthur Drummond had the ability to see an opening in a market, and with that true British spirit of enterprise formed a company to make lathes for model engineering.

Arthur Drummond was a talented artist and a self-taught engineer. In 1898, he constructed his own lathe in his workshop at his home in Pinks Hill near Guildford. Fellow engineering enthusiasts were impressed, so with £5,000 capital he and his brother went into business.

In 1902 they introduced their first production lathes from their new premises at Rydes Hill.

Working the furnaces at Drummond Bros.

The yard at Drummond Bros with a stockpile of components.

Arthur was the driving force behind the business, and with his numerous designs the product range was adapted to suit the ever-changing demands of the market place. Its 4in cylindrical-bed model-makers' lathe was sold for £5, making it within the financial reach of the average person. Motor garages also used these lathes, and a Drummond lathe was onboard Captain Scott's ship on his ill-fated trip to the South Pole.

In 1912, Arthur visited Australia and on his return he invented the Colonial Lathe. It could be used to repair boring tubes for artesian wells.

In a short time Drummond Bros became the first choice for model-makers throughout the world, with agents in Russia, Japan, India and Argentina.

The firm was pressed into work for the armed forces during World War One, coming under direct Government control in 1915. Drummond lathes made for the Royal Navy proved to be very reliable when worked in harsh conditions. The army also installed them in mobile workshops.

A fire at the factory in 1915 destroyed about 80 percent of the buildings, along with most of its records.

After the war, a flood of surplus machine tools affected the sale of new machines. As an interim measure, the management widened the firm's range of products under the Willing Worker name. These included a lightweight concrete mixer, power saw, pumps and a house lighting set. All of these were powered by the Willing Worker three-horsepower stationary engine. In 1924, lawn mowers were added to the brand, but they were not so successful.

During this period and into the 1930s, Drummonds built on its success with some clever advertising that not only showed its whole range of machine tools, but the actual items that could be made with them. One was a full-size car made by a Mr W. Taylor!

In fact, the growing motor industry demanded high-production turning equipment for making its components. Drummonds rose to the challenge, introducing a lathe that was the first of its kind in the UK – the Number 1 Maxicut. The Austin motor works in Birmingham was the first factory to have one installed in 1926.

Birmingham became the site for Drummond Sales Ltd. This was run by a new director, Arthur Andrews. This new venture led to an arrangement with William Asquith Ltd, who in turn became the sole selling agent for Drummonds' products in the UK.

Gear-cutting machines were introduced in 1932, and these too were used throughout the motor and aircraft industries.

For the duration of World War Two, the Ministry of Supply ordered the company to stop making small machine tools for use by model engineers. Production was taken over by Myfords, which is still a leading manufacturer of such machines.

Wartime work at Drummonds was for military contracts that included cranks and propeller shafts for the Bristol aircraft engine being cut on Drummonds' own Maxicut No. 2 lathe.

Arthur Drummond retired from the board of directors in 1946 and died in 1951 at the age of 86. His successor was George Hickman, who had started as an apprentice with the firm in its early days. He went on to serve the company for 60 years.

The company's share capital was taken over by the Asquith Machine Company in 1953. Thirteen years later it became the Drummond Division of Staveley Machine Tools Ltd.

Halcyon days in the post-war era brought further expansion. The workforce was increased to more than 300 in the 1960s, and it ran a first-class apprenticeship scheme.

Employees were well looked after, many of them working there for several decades. It was not unusual for half of the Portsmouth train to be booked for the works' summer outing.

The 1970s saw lathes made at Rydes Hill being shipped to the ZIL Car plant in Moscow, as part of a £14 million installation of an automated production line.

The company's fortunes began to slide in 1977 with a disastrous project known as the Multi-turn 200 lathe. It was an automatic machine with an early type of computer control. The firm went ahead

The Friary Meux brewery as seen from Commercial Road.

Women busy in the bottling department.

After describing beer as an extract of malted barley, boiled with hops and fermented with yeast; and noting that the word 'water' is never spoken at the brewery, only the word 'liquor', he mentioned the grinding machine that handled the barley. It was under the care of Dudley Bushell, who had been working there for 13 years.

He then met Mr M.F. Buchanan, a white-coated brewer, who was regulating the inflow of tons of ground grain into the mash tuns. A Mr I.A. Dennis was weighing hops, some from as far away as Yugoslavia, and some from as near as Runfold near Farnham. Most, however, were from the Kent hop gardens.

Looking after three steaming copper cauldrons, each holding more than 8,000 gallons of boiling liquor, was Stan Sims. After boiling came the cooling process and the visitor was then shown the department known as the tun rooms, where fermentation and refrigeration took place. Here he met the assistant foreman Bill Wiles. Meanwhile, foreman Reg Ricketts was testing a brew for its gravity. Under his command were 144,000 gallons of beer.

Beer for bottling was stored in tanks, which reminded the writer of ships' boilers. He wrote that foreman Tom Coombes 'is surrounded by dials, and as he paces his "deck"' he knows that his temperatures must be correct for beer which is later to be bottled and amounts to 1,600 gallons'.

In the racking department, which the writer described as like watching 'gigantic blood transfusions with snake-like pipes leading into casks', he met foreman John Picknell and his assistant Ernie Wiles. Next was the cooperage department, in which the foreman, Harold Oldham, was making wooden casks in the traditional manner. He told the reporter that his father and grandfather had also been coopers.

The brewery's 'sniffer' at work that day was John Loftus. He said: 'I smell each cask before it goes out for filling and also shine a light inside to make sure it is in a sweet-smelling condition. Sour smelling casks are thrown out.'

Barbara Seymour and Angela Etherington were in the bottling department. The writer watched Barbara seize four quart bottles at a time, 'smacking them into wooden crates and Angela helped her to speed them on their journey for thirsty customers'.

The Friary Meux had a sports ground at the Hazels at Pitch Place off the Worplesdon Road. It stored its wooden crates there at the times of the year when they were not needed.

Ash trays and a beer mat advertising Friary Meux Treble Gold.

Lastly, in the brewery's laboratory, the writer met five white-coated brewers – Messers Storey (head brewer), Crawford, Buchanan, Rogers and Howes, 'who, with scientific equipment, take samples from each barrel and check whether it is palatable'.

The last brew at Friary Meux in Guildford took place on 23 December 1968. It marked the end of the art of brewing that had gone on in the town for centuries.

The brewery's island site between Commercial Road, Onslow Street and North Street was then sold to MEPC for development.

It was with some sadness that many people gathered in Bridge Street and Commercial Road one Sunday morning in 1974 to see the Friary's landmark, its brewery tower, come crashing to the ground in a controlled explosion. It was as if those present were mourning an old friend who had been subject to an accident of the times.

The brewery certainly had a character all of its own, and if the redevelopment of the Friary shopping centre had occurred a decade later, with new ideas on town planning, sections of it may well have been kept and incorporated into the new centre. There were some gains, however, as the clearing of the site and the subsequent archaeological digs that took place revealed a great deal about the town's mediaeval past and the Dominican friary that once stood there.

A pub was incorporated into the new shopping centre and a competition was held to name it. The judges included the then editor of the *Surrey Advertiser*, Ted Adams, and Friary Meux' regional director, Julian Cartwright. (By this time Allied Breweries owned the Friary Meux name, but the beer was being brewed as far away as Romford in Essex). Two people came up with what was chosen as the winning name – the Blackfriars. They were Sid Elston, who served the town for many years at the Citizens' Advice Bureau, and a former employee of Friary Meux, Joe Perira.

The Blackfriars opened in 1981, but within seven years had closed, as part of a revamp of the centre to create more shops. It must be one of the shortest-lived pubs in the town.

Friary Meux beer bottles and a Pipkin Draught Bitter can. Friary Meux, in conjunction with the Metal Box Company, was one of the first breweries in the UK to use these seven-pint cans.

George Moreton with his horse-drawn delivery van of Chaplins Ltd, seen here in Bedford Road.

Waited on daily

Go back 50-odd years and there was a veritable army of delivery men (and women) calling on a daily basis in the Guildford area.

The milkman and the coalman will instantly spring to mind. But there were grocers, bakers, butchers and even egg farmers who brought their goods right to people's front doors; not to forget travelling shops that sold all kinds of provisions, and even fish and chip vans.

Some traders still used horse-drawn vehicles. When, for example, Frank Chew, the greengrocer from Ludlow Road, was seen entering a street on his horse-drawn cart, there was a distinct clatter of buckets and coal shovels. Householders who enjoyed growing flowers and vegetables rushed out in the hope of scooping up some manure for their gardens.

Even at this time, horses used by one Guildford dairy were still stabled in the town centre. There was a large stable yard in Stoke Road, nearly opposite what was then the milk bottling plant. The distinct smell of hay and steam from the manure was particularly pungent on cold frosty mornings.

Paper boys outside Whitehurst's general store in Manor Road, Stoughton, in the late 1930s.

In the 1950s, the big three dairymen were Lymposs & Smee, Home Counties Dairies and the Co-op, with Mead Bros' Dairy at Christmas Hill in Shalford. Go back a few years and there was the Stoke Hill & Lee Farm Dairy with its head office in Merrow, while Burden's sold bottled milk from its farm at Stoughton. White's Farm at One Tree Hill also sold milk and cream.

Chaplins Ltd was a general carrier with horse-drawn vehicles that was based at the Station Approach.

Larger stores such as Charles Holden Ltd, the Guildford Stores, Sainsbury's and the Co-op offered a delivery service. Orders were made up in store and vans or delivery boys were dispatched with the goods.

The delivery boys rode bikes with a small front wheel, above which was a large carrier. As well as the larger stores, just about every corner shop had one or more of these bicycles. As soon as school finished for the day, boys would be seen out delivering merchandise. They would earn about five shillings a week for this chore, and some had to carry quite heavy loads for several miles.

There was an instance when a young lad was carrying at least 28lb of sugar and a side of bacon on his delivery bike from the grocery wholesalers Stephenson & Sons, which had its premises in Castle Street.

One of Lymposs & Smee's horse-drawn milk floats, possibly decorated for a carnival and seen outside the dairy's High Street premises. Charlie Brewser is standing on the float with Basil Knapp next to him.

Charlie Brewser standing next to an electric milk float. He always greeted his customers with the words 'good morning' and a military-style salute.

As he rode down Guildford High Street and applied the brakes, he suddenly found the back end of the bike rising into the air. This was caused by the sheer weight in the front basket. It was with some difficulty, and with the help of a passing pedestrian, that he was able to gain control again. Stephenson & Sons were wholesale grocers who supplied the multitude of small town grocery shops.

Some of the night-shift workers at Plastic Coatings.

Originally called Durable Plastics, it was the brainchild of Nigel Vinson, now Baron Vinson of Roddam Dene, Northumberland.

Born in 1931 in Kent, Nigel Vinson went to Pangbourne Naval College but opted out of university mainly because of his hatred of Latin, which was a requirement at both Oxford and Cambridge. In his own words he preferred to 'get on with life'. However, at Pangbourne he had become interested in the technology used by a small plastics firm he visited with the school's science society.

After National Service with the Queen's Royal Regiment, he got a job working on the production line of the plastics firm Creators Ltd, of Woking. While there he noticed that the firm was under-using its system of PVC coating. With a windfall of £10,000 left to him after his parents had divorced, he soon set up his own firm, and with the help of a neighbour, 'Squiz' Squires, they developed a machine based on the technology Nigel Vinson had learned.

Nigel Vinson was 21 years of age when his company was registered on 18 September 1952. Its first break came within two months, with an order to supply equipment to Hoover for its washing machines. Within four years, the company was employing 25 people.

In 1956, the company moved to a purpose-built factory at Woodbridge Meadows and within a few years other factories were opened in Farnham in Surrey, at Winsford in Cheshire, Kingswinford in Staffordshire and at Harpenden in Hertfordshire.

Many household and industrial items – from draining racks for crockery and kitchen utensils to industrial pipes, garden furniture and surgical instruments – are covered in a film of protective plastic. By the 1980s, three principal techniques were used – dipping into a tank of liquid, dipping into fine powder, and spraying.

The initial success of Plastic Coatings was due to it using the latest technology to combine the strength of metal – which, of course, tends to corrode – with the anti-corrosive properties of plastic. New markets were created as Plastic Coatings passed on its know-how to other companies throughout the world.

When the firm became a public limited company in 1969, Nigel Vinson showed his gratitude to his loyal staff by giving two-thirds of them 10 percent of the share value.

Plastic Coatings received the Queen's Award for Industry in 1971, and later that year it was acquired by Imperial Tobacco for £4.7 million. Nigel Vinson gave up the post of chairman the following year to become its non-executive chairman.

However, he already had thoughts of doing much more than being the head of a successful plastics firm. He became chairman of the Crafts Council in 1972 and was attracted to the Institute of Economic Affairs

The Rt Hon. Lord Vinson at his home in Northumberland, sitting on the seat made of stones that came from the arch above the entrance to Friary Square.

(IEA), as he was anxious to put back into a free market society the opportunity for others to have the same success that he had enjoyed. He also yearned to return to his family's farming roots, so he bought 4,500 acres of prime farmland on the Roddam and Hetton & Holborn Estates in Northumberland.

He served on the Silver Jubilee Appeal for four years as an honorary director, during which time the charity raised more than £16 million. Nigel Vinson then went on to see the expansion of Gatwick and Stansted airports as a director of British Airports Authority. He was recommended to Sir Keith Joseph and Margaret Thatcher for his interests in the philosophy of the IEA and went on to set up and also manage the Centre for Policy Studies.

A long list of other chairmanships included being head of the Rural Development Commission and holding a number of directorships which included Barclays Bank.

Part of the proceeds of the sale of his company went into a charity that supported many causes, including that of freedom of expression.

He was awarded a life peerage in 1984 and was soon willing to take on worthy causes, one of which was the right of Sikhs to wear turbans instead of crash helmets when riding motorcycles.

In 1995, Lord Vinson was made a Deputy Lieutenant of Northumberland, an honour to a newcomer that pleased him immensely. And a bit of old Guildford has made its way to his estate. After the former militia barracks were demolished, the stones that made up the arch ended up with an antiques dealer – believed to be Granshaw's of Shalford.

When Nigel Vinson retired as chairman of Plastic Coatings in 1973, the stones were purchased by the firm and presented to him as a leaving present. They form a very attractive semi-circular seat on a hillside at Roddam Hall.

The factory at Woodbridge Meadows closed in 2006 and has since been demolished. However, International Process Technologies Limited, the parent company of Plastic Coatings Limited, continues to operate successfully in Farnham, Surrey, and Rotterdam in the Netherlands, and at PLC factories offering coating services based at Risca in South Wales and at Kingswinford in the West Midlands.

CHAPTER FIVE

MARKET TOWN TO REGIONAL CENTRE

On Stag Hill

Stag Hill was being farmed right up to the decade before the University of Surrey was built there.

In 1954, the harvest was gathered in true turn-of-the-20th-century fashion. Young people, including students from Guildford Technical College, helped out, earning about one shilling and sixpence an hour.

Stag Hill was part of Guildford Park Farm. The farmer was Mr Baldry, who had a cereal crop to harvest. The mechanical reaper used on the farm had been made before World War One and had been designed to be pulled by a horse. Now at its head was a Fordson tractor. As it was pulled along it cut the corn and dropped it as wheat sheaves.

The casual workers' job was to pick up the sheaves, two at a time under each arm, and push the corn heads together so that they stood off the ground in the form of a stook.

This task took a little time to perfect, but once completed they formed a pleasant backdrop to the countryside, right on the edge of Guildford town centre. The sheaves of corn were left standing for several days until all the cutting was completed.

Pitching, the next stage, was also achieved after some practice. The aim was to place the pitch fork just below the binding on the sheaf, and with one swing, land it squarely on to the cart. There, a colleague would load it with care. A badly loaded wagon could easily cause a serious accident.

It was equally important to avoid the possibility of stabbing the loader with a pitchfork – as most of the time he was out of sight.

The corn was cut from the edge of the field, gradually working towards the centre. Tension mounted as the patch left in the middle slowly became smaller and smaller. This was the last refuge for the odd rabbit or rat. At the very last moment any animal that remained there would make a break for freedom, while having to run the gauntlet of an enthusiastic terrier dog.

Work started in the fields as soon after dawn as possible, but it was important to let the morning dew on the corn dry, to avoid the formation of mildew.

Weather permitting, work continued until dusk. The farmer did not allow the casual workers to strip to the waist in hot weather, in case they suffered sunburn and then went off sick. Too much liquid was not allowed either, as the farmer believed this would weaken the labourer.

An aerial view of Stag Hill with the cathedral nearing completion. Note the fields extending to the railway line at the top of the picture. The University of Surrey now covers the area.

A new diluted orange drink, called Sun Crush, was popular. It appeared to have remnants of real oranges in it. Lunch breaks were taken in the fields. Food was usually tomato sandwiches, which, by that time of the day, had become rather soggy.

On the southern slope of Stag Hill there was a rather smelly area where pigs were kept and also a muddy duck pond. Near here were two steel-clad farm workers' bungalows. They had been erected in 1925 as an experiment by the owner of Stag Hill and Guildford Park Farm, the Earl of Onslow. It is believed that the bungalows survived until about the 1970s.

The outside covering consisted of mild-steel plates one-eighth of an inch thick, screwed to a 4in x 2in wooden frame. The roof was made of red asbestos cement slates laid on top of a felt lining. They were manufactured and erected by the Glasgow-based firm of G. & J. Weir Ltd.

The semi-detached pair each had two bedrooms, a living room, scullery, larder, coal cellar, bathroom and lavatory. Access to all rooms was via an entrance lobby. The pair cost Lord Onslow a

A view across the fields from Stag Hill, looking north towards the Dennis Bros factory and on towards Stoughton.

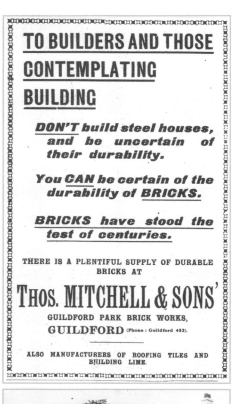

TO BUILDERS AND THOSE CONTEMPLATING BUILDING

DON'T build steel houses, and be uncertain of their durability.

You *CAN* be certain of the durability of **BRICKS.**

BRICKS have stood the test of centuries.

THERE IS A PLENTIFUL SUPPLY OF DURABLE BRICKS AT

THOS. MITCHELL & SONS'

GUILDFORD PARK BRICK WORKS,

GUILDFORD (Phone : Guildford 453).

ALSO MANUFACTURERS OF ROOFING TILES AND BUILDING LIME.

This local newspaper advertisement was placed by brick manufacturer Thomas Mitchell & Sons warning builders not to build steel houses owing to the uncertainty of their durability.

The iron–clad bungalows at Guildford Park Farm soon after they had been erected in 1925.

The University of Surrey takes shape in the 1960s on what was once fields at Stag Hill.

little more than £1,000. They were fitted out with a gas stove and gas boiler, a tub and a sink in the scullery, and with electric lighting throughout.

Set on a concrete base, work on them commenced on 2 July 1925 and was completed for a grand opening just over a month later on 17 August. A large crowd of representatives from local councils turned up, along with others interested in this new-fangled way of building houses. It was said that to build a similar sized dwelling in brick and traditional materials would have taken four months.

This took place at a time when demand outstripped the availability of homes for ordinary working people. There was also a shortage of materials and skilled labour.

In giving his speech at the opening of the steel-clad bungalows, the Earl of Onslow remarked that the building trade was trying to employ one apprentice to every three skilled men, but it would take time before the number of trained craftsmen increased.

He said he had decided to do something about the housing shortage and difficulties in the building trade by experimenting with these bungalows, although, he pointed out, their system of construction 'could not in any way be considered to replace bricks and mortar and concrete, but perhaps they might stop the gap created by the shortage owing to the war'.

He added that more about the usefulness of the bungalows would be known in the next year after the tenants had lived in them for 12 months.

It was somewhat ironic that the steel-clad bungalows were erected close to Thomas Mitchell & Sons' Guildford Park Brickworks.

In the *Surrey Times* of 22 August 1925, in which there was a lengthy report on the opening of the bungalows, the brickmaker Thomas Mitchell took out an advertisement that was a direct attack on the idea of building homes with unconventional materials.

It stated: 'To builders and those contemplating building. Don't build steel houses, and be uncertain of their durability. You can be certain of the durability of bricks. Bricks have stood the test of centuries. There is a plentiful supply of durable bricks at Thos.Mitchell & Sons.'

However, these temporary homes, a kind of early version of the prefabricated homes introduced in answer to the acute housing shortage at the end of World War Two, remained in use for a lot longer than the Earl of Onslow may have imagined. But it is said that they were quite damp and not very comfortable.

Guildford Cathedral

As early as the reign of Henry VIII, it was suggested that Guildford should have a cathedral. But it was not until Surrey became a garden suburb of London, thanks to the railways, bringing a migration from the south of the capital, that it was found that the Diocese of Winchester needed to be divided to accommodate the increased numbers in the new commuter belt.

The Diocese of Guildford was formed in 1927 with its first bishop the Right Revd John Harold Greig. He was enthroned in Holy Trinity Church in Guildford High Street on 12 July of that year. The church then became the cathedral church of the new diocese.

Bishop Greig's challenge was to establish this new diocese. He did this with much zeal until ill health forced him to lay down his crosier seven years later.

The new diocese required additional churches to be built. In Guildford alone three new churches were built, all very close to the cathedral. They are: St Francis' at Westborough, All Saints' at Onslow Village, and St Clare's Church at Park Barn.

The architect of Guildford Cathedral, Sir Edward Maufe.

Bishop Greig also believed in taking the word of the Lord to the people. He organised large outdoor services in places such as Newlands Corner, Frensham Ponds and at Hindhead.

But what was needed most for the new diocese was its own cathedral. In 1933 the Earl of Onslow gave the site on the top of Stag Hill, but the sides of the hill were to be auctioned. This worried the diocese as, if it was outbid, access to its site may have been made difficult. However, in 1947, a former prime minister of Canada, Viscount Bennett of Calgary and Mickleham, stepped forward and purchased the hill for £10,000, and gifted it to the people of Guildford.

The cathedral was to be, to use a phrase at the time, 'a jewel set in an emerald sea'.

A competition for the new building was held in 1932 and the winning architect was Edward Maufe. His design was the first interpretation of contemporary Gothic and indeed is only the second new cathedral in England to be built on an entirely new site since the Middle Ages. The other is Liverpool Cathedral. Maufe was later knighted for his design.

In Sir Edward's design, the reinforced walls of the nave made the need for buttresses unnecessary.

The Cathedral Church of the Holy Spirit – to give Guildford Cathedral its full title – stands on an ideal east-west escarpment, some 440 feet above sea level. The internal length is 365 feet, and it was designed to seat 1,700 people. It is approximately the same size as Exeter Cathedral, but its nave, at 41 feet wide, is second only to York Minster at 44 feet.

The foundation stone was laid on 22 July 1936 by the then Archbishop of Canterbury, Dr Cosmo Gordon Lang. The stone can be seen opposite the entrance to the Lady Chapel at the east end of the building. The stone rests on fragments of stone taken from both Winchester and Canterbury cathedrals.

Building work progressed fairly well until the outbreak of World War Two in 1939.

At the time it was feared that the unfinished building might become a target for the Luftwaffe – especially after Hitler ordered the bombing of other cathedral cities such as Canterbury and Coventry. It was, of course, spared. But there is a theory that it was not targeted as it proved a useful marker for German aircraft en route to and from London.

Building work resumed after the war but petered out due to a lack of funds in 1951. It was restarted in the mid-1950s, largely due to the efforts of a remarkable women, Eleonora Iredale. She was secretary of the New Cathedral Fund, although she suffered from almost hostile reticence at times from the people around her. When she retired from the post in 1962, she had been responsible for raising about £660,000.

A vitriolic speech in 1954, by the then Mayor of Guildford, the Labour councillor Leslie Codd, to a diocesan conference also went some way to getting the project back on track. He was deeply worried by the lack of urgency in the building project of those he was addressing. He told them that they 'had to build it, or sell it – to become something like a furniture depository'.

It was not long before the Buy a Brick Campaign was launched to raise money to buy the one million bricks needed to complete the nave.

Bricks and brick tokens were sold for two shillings and sixpence. It certainly helped to raise the cathedral's profile and money poured in by way of other donations as well.

The Queen and Prince Philip visited the cathedral in the summer of 1957 to see how work was progressing, and nearly four years later, on 17 May 1961, they returned for the consecration of the Cathedral Church of the Holy Spirit. However, work on the tower was not finished until the mid-1960s.

Guildford Cathedral as it looked in the early 1950s before the nave was built.

Work is progressing well with the nave nearly finished and just the tower to be completed.

How many people walking in the nave and aisles know that the stone that they are walking upon is the same stone as that used in the Colliseum in Rome? It is, of course, a stone known as travertine. The Queen's Chapel is graced by Ashburton marble from Devon, while in the Children's Chapel, the green marble comes from Sweden.

It was always intended to make the building, unlike its mediaeval forebears, light and uncluttered. For that purpose the windows on the north side were to be clear. However, if you look carefully you will see a series of small stars.

Those working on the roof would have had a fantastic view of the surrounding countryside.

This was a puzzle at first, but when questioned, Sir Edward Maufe replied that there was no special meaning. He said that he just liked stars. How many visitors have found the architect's signature stone? To give a clue: it is on the south side.

The majority of the coatings on the outside of the building were handmade at the brickworks that was just down the hill at Guildford Park.

There are six miles of copper piping set in the concrete under the marble floor.

When requests for needleworkers to decorate kneelers were made in the 1950s, it was quite a surprise that so much skill was still practised within the diocese. There are nearly 2,000 kneelers. Each is a unique design and each one has been individually worked.

Unfortunately, Guildford Cathedral can no longer be described as a jewel in an emerald sea. The expansion of the town over the past 40-odd years has meant that the sprawl of the University of Surrey on the north side unfortunately does little to enhance the cathedral's appearance.

The diocese has unveiled plans to develop around the cathedral with more of its own buildings. Another ambitious idea is to dig into the hill itself to create an underground car park. The upkeep of the building is massive and schemes such as these, if completed, would bring in much-needed revenue.

Sir Edward Maufe's bold architectural statement still raises differences of opinion. Guildfordians seem divided between those who believe that it looks more like a power station, and those who applaud it as a rare and beautiful example of 20th-century British architecture.

A view across the rooftops of the town in the late 1930s. Twenty years later a number of new buildings would begin to dominate the skyline.

Future plans

It was 1944 and the war was not yet won. Although the Allies had landed in France, in the Home Counties we had the terror of the V1 and V2 rockets that came out of those clear blue skies with little or no warning.

However, Guildford was already making plans for its future in the years of peace that were expected to come. In July 1946, the document *Guildford of the Future* was finally served up to residents, who longed for a 'brave new world'.

The plan was drawn up by a well-known and respected planning consultant, G.A. Jellicoe, in the spirit of Sir Patrick Abercrombie's Greater London Plan.

Now, 60 years on, it makes interesting reading to see what has and hasn't come about. It must be pointed out that at the time Guildford was still seen as a fairly small and self-contained market town. Now, it is seen by many as an important regional centre for the south-east of England.

Back in 1946, the plan envisaged was that the population would increase from 45,000 to 53,000. The town centre would be the epicentre of both business and culture and would serve an area way beyond the Guildford boundary of the time.

Looking down from the tower of St Nicolas' Church towards the Town Bridge. The buildings on either side of the High Street next to the river would be demolished to make way for the town's gyratory road system.

The arts were to play an important part in this new plan. Music was regarded as being especially important. An open-air venue would be created which would also attract the best of sport – cricket being especially favoured.

However, as borough councillor Leslie Codd pointed out at the time, there would, in fact, be no sizeable outside sports stadium.

Most importantly, it was decreed that Guildford should have a spiritual quality. To help that need, more use should be made of a precinct at the site of the then unfinished cathedral at Stag Hill, with a new road running to it from the town.

Another view from St Nicolas' Church, this time looking up The Mount in the days before yellow lines and parking restrictions.

It was planned that Guildford would have five distinct neighbourhoods: Stoughton, Bellfields, Onslow, Merrow and Burpham. These would be small townships, completely self-contained dormitories, with their own shops and community buildings. They would have their own schools, complete with playing fields, as well as public playing fields and open spaces.

Downland, such as on the Hog's Back, should be kept green, and be allowed to penetrate as far into the town centre as Green Lane does today.

The plan stated that Stag Hill, the home of Guildford Cathedral, should remain green to magnify the majesty of 'this contemporary gothic building'. In fact, the report waxes lyrical about the aesthetic possibilities of the Stag Hill site. It even suggested that cattle could be grazed on the slopes, provided that this did not cause the residents any great concern!

The report suggested that the river and water meadows be used as much as possible for recreational use, as well as remaining scenic. It was believed that this would make the town centre a pleasant place in which to both live and work.

It was proposed that the town centre should also have a special industrial zone for selected light industry, together with a business zone.

Stoke Park was thought to be more useful for the proposed school programme, and more use was to be made of the adjoining water meadows for public recreation.

To progress this school programme further, the report suggested the removal of the Royal Grammar School from its outdated original home in the upper High Street to a site at Stoke Park. The old school building would then become a museum with gardens around it.

Foxenden Quarry, now a multi-storey car park, was suggested as a site for an open-air theatre which would prove popular as the acoustics were thought to be good.

It was suggested that the present A3 should become a local road with a new arterial road following a new route.

Like now, traffic approaching Guildford from the north became tangled with the normal town centre traffic. As such, a further orbital road to bypass this problem was thought to be necessary. This was still being discussed until the highways came under the auspices of Surrey County Council in the 1970s. The proposed road was too expensive, so the county council went for a cheaper option, which is the town's present gyratory system. It can be argued that it did little for Guildford except to cut one of the most beautiful high streets in the country in two.

It was also suggested that what is now Parkway, beside Stoke Park, and all similar roads, should enjoy a speed limit of 15mph.

Three new railway stations were proposed for the outskirts of the town, each with large car parks. An airport, however, was ruled out in this report, which went on to suggest that it might be possible to build a helicopter pad adjacent to York Road or indeed at the main railway station.

Tunsgate and the car park on the site that would later be developed as a shopping mall.

The report stated that Sydenham Road had potential if it was widened so as to relieve pressure on traffic passing through the upper High Street. It was admitted that it would mean the loss of some interesting buildings, but the new view of the castle that would emerge was thought to make the scheme worthwhile.

Quarry Street would also need attention, so as to ease traffic on its way towards Shalford.

The site of what became Guildford Civic Hall would have housed a new assize court.

Guildford's 'Cinderella street', North Street, was to be left to its own salvation, mainly as the fruit and veg market was held there.

The former power station, today's Electric Theatre, was to be kept as it was believed it could be converted to produce atomic power!

These were the bare bones of the proposal put to the full council in those dark and austere days of the mid-1940s. Since then, a proposed central bus station has been adopted. We have an urban motorway, although back then the word 'motorway' was not used as such, and instead these roads were described as a 'road operating as a rail system'.

The plan received cautious approval, but a lack of funds hindered much being done at first. Besides, councillors did not wish to impose an increase on the rates.

The 1959 election

The well-known paraphrased remark 'you've never had it so good!', made by prime minister Harold 'Supermac' Macmillan, dates from the time of the 1959 general election. And the battle for the Parliamentary seat in Guildford that year was one of the most memorable of any held in the constituency.

It was a three-way fight between the Conservative's Richard 'Dick' Nugent, who held the seat, Bill Bellerby for Labour, and Major Arthur Braybrooke for the Liberal party.

There had been some shuffling of the political parties in the UK and this added to the drama that was about to unfold.

Dick Nugent MP and his wife Ruth out campaigning. After retaining the Guildford seat for the Conservatives in the 1959 election, he held on to it at the elections in 1964 and 1966, stepping down in 1970 when David Howell was elected.

The Tories had been fighting elections under the name of the Conservative, Unionist and Liberal Party. As a result of Labour's landslide general election victory of 1945, leading Liberals had agreed to join the Tories as they felt to remain independent would help the Labour Party to remain in power.

In Guildford, a letter of declaration was signed by leading Liberals in the town. These included Mr R.M. Hardy of Stan Hardy men's outfitters, Mr A.W. Graham Brown, Harold Gammon of Gammons department store, and Mr C.E. Nicklin. However, the decision was not supported by the Liberal chairman, Mr P.B. Smith.

It seems that most local Liberals were eventually remustered under the new banner in their fight to defeat socialism.

However, by the 1959 general election there was a resurgence of Liberalism across the UK. Pressure was put on the Tories to drop the name 'Liberal' from their title, and with reluctance they did so after a further statement by the signatories of the 1948 declaration, which stated that they would stay with the name 'Conservative Party'.

In the run-up to the election that October, the Tories were nervous, but a keen campaign followed. Issues of the time,

The Labour candidate Bill Bellerby at the time of the 1959 election.

The picture and story that appeared on the front page of the *Surrey Times* after the result of the Guildford seat was announced from the balcony of the Guildhall.

From their smiles you might think they'd all just been elected to Parliament. The only ones not smiling are Mrs. Bellerby, leaning against the door-post (her husband had just lost two thousand votes) and Mr. Gilbert Futter, just behind her (he's the Mayor's secretary and that's no laughing matter, even though the Mayor, in the background, is laughing). It's the scene on the balcony of Guildford Guildhall as the Deputy Acting Returning Officer, Mr. H. C. Weller read the results. Left to right the party are: Mrs. Nugent; Mr. Dick Nugent, still M.P.; Mr. Weller; the Mayor (Ald. C. E. Nicklin); Mr. Bill Bellerby, the Labour candidate; Mr. Futter; Mrs. Bellerby; Major Braybrooke, the Liberal candidate; and Mrs. Braybrooke.

[Photo: D. E. F. Eldridge.]

such as 'worry about the bomb' and old-age pensions, came to the fore. But interestingly, the question of the Common Market did not play a part in any party's manifesto.

Several years before, local young activists held their own mock Guildford Parliament in the former Guildford House in the upper High Street. Two of the candidates who stood for Guildford in 1959, Dick Nugent and Bill Bellerby, had been members of that local 'parliament'.

Dick Nugent was a farmer from Dunsfold who had been adopted as the Tory's candidate in 1947. Much respected, he and his wife, Ruth, never forgot a face. At meetings, she always made a note of people they met and a short résumé of their conversation. She also made notes on what she was wearing at the time.

Schoolteacher Bill Bellerby had made his home in Guildford after serving in the Queen's Royal Regiment during the war. He had done his teacher training in his native South Wales and at the time of the election was deputy headmaster at Woodlands County Primary School at Sheerwater, Woking.

The Liberal candidate was Major Arthur Braybrooke, who lived in Cranleigh. He was a product of the Royal Military Academy, Sandhurst, and saw service in India after being seconded to the RAF as an Army Co-operation pilot. At one point he resigned his commission and was ordained into the Church of England, but he rejoined the colours in 1939.

The Major was a renowned cricketer and had played rugby for Gloucester. He had been awarded a triple Blue for cricket, rugby and hockey. He was also a former Tory, and had sat on the Conservative's Central Board of Finance.

All three adopted entirely different campaign techniques. Dick Nugent followed the traditional Tory line of public meetings in village and church halls, while Bill Bellerby preferred open meetings and whistle-stop visits.

Major Braybrooke adopted a novel approach by serenading shoppers with a Tommy Steel-style guitar routine.

All canvassed the housing estates in Guildford, with Bill Bellerby experiencing one rather awkward situation. When calling on one woman she slammed the door in his face.

Bill knocked on the door again. In fact he actually knocked on the door many times before the woman reappeared at the window and told him to go away. Bill assured her that he would go away if she would only reopen the front door as his raincoat was trapped in it!

Election day came and, when the polls closed, the local parties retired to Guildford Technical College where the votes were counted.

There was an 80 percent turnout, with Dick Nugent holding on to the seat. He polled 27,198 votes, only 85 more than the last election in 1955.

Labour's Bill Bellerby came next with 13,756, a drop of 2,000 votes on the previous general election. The new Liberal candidate, Major Arthur Braybrooke, polled 6,318 votes, which showed at that time the lost Labour votes went to the Liberals and not the Tories.

The relieved Dick Nugent, not to be upstaged by Major Braybrooke and his guitar act, struck up a chorus of *To Be A Farmer's Boy*.

So started the long Liberal challenge for the Guildford seat, which was finally won from the Tories in 1999, only to be regained by them in 2004.

Perhaps one could say that Bill Bellerby was the best MP that Guildford never had. He and his wife Doreen have given Guildfordians decades of sterling service, serving as borough and county councillors while doing many other good things for the community. For that they have received the highest honour their adopted town could bestow upon them – freedom of the borough of Guildford.

The Buchanan report

During the early 1960s, Guildford had become Surrey's new boom town, with its newly opened civic hall, department stores and multi-storey car park in Sydenham Road.

The building of the car park caused a good deal of concern, as it took away the garden of the County Club. However, there were genuine fears when the building group Richard Costains applied to build a multi-storey office block within the approach to the railway station.

Richard Costains's plan was refused,

Bridge House, on the corner of Bridge Street and Walnut Tree Close, was one of the town's 'boom town' buildings. Built in the early 1960s, it was gone by the end of the 1980s.

In 1964 there were plans for a multi-storey office block here at the Station Approach. The saga went to a public inquiry and what was described at the time as 'Guildford's skyscraper' was never built.

Guildford railway station and its car park in the 1960s.

but if the office block had been built, it might well have brought valuable rail-bound commuters into the town. Granted, Bridge House was built near the station at the end of Walnut Tree Close, but so many workers and visitors pouring into Guildford were now coming by car.

The borough council approached the firm of Colin Buchanan & Partners, whose staff had produced the seminal *Traffic in Towns* report for the Government, for its opinion on the growing traffic problem within central Guildford. When it published its findings in 1965, it came as a surprise to many that the borough had only been thinking as far ahead as 1981 with regard to the town's traffic. Colin Buchanan & Partners believed the council should have planned until at least the end of the 20th century.

The main aims of the report were to separate pedestrian traffic from motor traffic. It was found that much heavy traffic ended up in the town centre, when its main aim was to pass through.

What the town really needed was a road running north-south to relieve the congestion. Two routes were, however, proposed. One was a bypass to the north of the town, branching off the A3 at Burpham, and the second was a road running south around the town in the Bramley area.

However, a certain amount of traffic relief in the town centre was achieved almost by accident. During the 1960s it was necessary to introduce a temporary one-way system along certain streets, such as Quarry Street, while major road maintenance work was undertaken. So successful was this temporary measure that it was adopted permanently.

Despite Colin Buchanan & Partners' report, Guildford's north-south road plan was put on hold. The idea began to fade when, in the 1990s, the Government ruled that no new road schemes would be allowed. It can be argued that the effect of this has enabled the University of Surrey to expand towards Manor Farm, where a relief road could have been constructed.

However, it could be said that the north-south road concept was really buried at the time when Surrey County Council became

Road improvements in Park Street in the 1970s.

The former technical college building in Park Street being demolished at the end of the 1960s.

The town's gyratory road system under construction. The scheme included a new bridge over the river.

responsible for the county's highways following an act of Parliament in 1972. The county council opted for the present gyratory system in the town centre which, over the years, has had many critics.

The Buchanan report on Guildford's traffic situation contained some observations that, more than 40 years on, can be viewed as rather interesting. For example, the report put great emphasis on maintaining the Guildford to Cranleigh railway line, which, at the time, was about to close as a result of the Beeching cuts.

Lost buildings

Post-war Guildford, like most UK towns, embarked on a programme of demolishing buildings to make way for new developments.

It was a time of bold new ideas and in many towns and cities large blocks of unsightly flats and offices sprang up. However, there was one saving grace for Guildfordians, as its planners tended to be slower in adopting these new ideas. They were late on the scene with the idea of tower blocks, which lost support after the gas explosion that ripped apart a section of Ronan Point, the 23-storey block of flats in east London, soon after they were occupied in 1968. The Mount Place flats are Guildford's highest such development from this period.

However, in Guildford several fine houses fell foul of the post-war purge on buildings which, it could be argued, were the bedrock of life in the town.

The Firs in London Road was one such fine house. It was acquired by the borough council in 1937, but became embroiled in a heated debate as to its value. At the time, that part of the town was deemed not suitable for shops.

The Firs was closeted from view by tall fir trees that surrounded it. Its demise became a public issue in the early 1950s as plans were being made to turn the site into a car park – pending the building of a new civic hall. The property remained empty, deteriorated, and was finally swept away.

Allen House, a little lower down the High Street, was another old and apparently much-liked building. Back in the 1950s, it was part of the Royal Grammar School (RGS) complex. However, the building was looking tired. Its future was also subject to a great debate, but it eventually made way for a new part of the RGS, which still occupies the site.

A rare glimpse of The Firs in London Road in the 1930s.

The demolition of the row of shops stretching from the RGS building down to the corner of North Street caused a great deal of outcry. The corner was known as Masseys Corner after the chemist shop run by the Massey family. Old Mr Massey used to spend a great a deal of time standing at his shop door telling his latest joke to those who would stop and listen.

The row of shops that now stands on the site was designed by John Brownrigg, built as a temporary project in the late 1950s.

Several of Guildford's old manor houses are now just memories. Stoke Park Mansion was one such building. It became run down and met an inappropriate end in 1977.

It had come into the borough's hands in the 1930s after being used as a private school. The building was used as a base for General Post Office Telephones and later as part of the teaching block serving Guildford Technical College.

Its end came quite quickly when a senior member of the college's staff noticed water trickling down a lighting fixture in the basement. A decision was swiftly taken to have it demolished.

The builder R. Holford & Co. has already put its sign up in front of Allen House in the upper High Street. It was demolished to make way for a new part of the Royal Grammar School.

The rear of Allen House at the time of its demolition.

Perhaps one of the most beautiful of Guildford's mansions was that at Stoke Hill, the former home of the Paynter family. Francis Paynter succeeded his father, Samuel, as rector of St John's Church, Stoke-next-Guildford. Francis's wife Julia, although referred to by many as Fanny, lived to the age of 99, passing away in 1939.

The Stoke Hill estate has become Bellfields, but at the time of its development there were plans to save Stoke Hill House and turn it into a community centre. This scheme never reached fruition. It was divided into flats during the acute housing shortage of the late 1940s and 50s, but soon after began to deteriorate and was pulled down. Right to the end it kept some of its former grace on its lofty hilltop position. Part of the old stable block and a high brick wall do remain.

Ardmore House in Stoughton suffered a similar fate. The only trace of its existence is the old gatekeeper's cottage at the bottom of Manor Road.

Seen from the tower of Holy Trinity Church is Masseys Corner at the junction of North Street and the upper High Street.

The loss of the old cottages in Park Street was a great disappointment. From the outside they were full of character, but evidently inside they had become very run down. Despite their quirkiness and historical value, the order of the day back then was not to conserve, but to demolish.

They had an overhanging eve on the first floor and at one time there were bus stops along that part of Park Street. Passengers could shelter from the rain under the eves of these cottages. In fact, people have been sheltering under similar eves for centuries. But while doing so, it has often been possible to hear a conversation within the house. It's where the term eavesdropping comes from.

Stoke Park Mansion met its date with the demolition men in 1977.

These ramshackle cottages in Park Street are now just a distant memory. If they had survived to this day they would have had a preservation order slapped on them.

North Street

North Street has never reached the same high status as the High Street, to which it runs parallel. However, at one time it was the 'workshop of the town centre' with many interesting businesses and shops.

It was the home of Pimms, a firm that was mainly involved with furnishings. It was also the town's main undertakers, complete with its own chapel of rest. Pimms made a variety of wood products on site including coffins for its 'temporary residents'. So adaptable was this unit

The Co-op was a prominent store that fronted North Street. Seen here are some of the staff during the 1940s.

that in the early 1950s Pimms made television cabinets for Peto Scott.

At the entrance to Pimms were two large wooden gates. On working days these closed at 5.30pm sharp and the doors of the Dolphin pub next door would open to refresh Pimms' employees after a hard day's work.

The demolition of the Dolphin could be argued as being another sad loss to the town. Evidently, the inside walls once had some unique murals painted on them.

Immediately past what was originally George Abbot's manufactory building, and which has seen many uses, including that of a school and now as a woollen shop, was tent maker Alfred Bull's premises. Today, the library occupies Bull's site.

The town's market moved from the High Street to North Street in 1865. This was because animal pens were restricting the movement of traffic in the High Street. The Tuesday cattle market moved to a purpose-built site in Woodbridge Road in 1896. But market stalls returned to North Street in 1919 to allow people who had begun to cultivate allotment gardens a place to sell their surplus produce. It was a time of dire food shortages following World War One and the council made land available and encouraged people to 'grow their own'.

It was not long before there was pressure from traders, both locally and

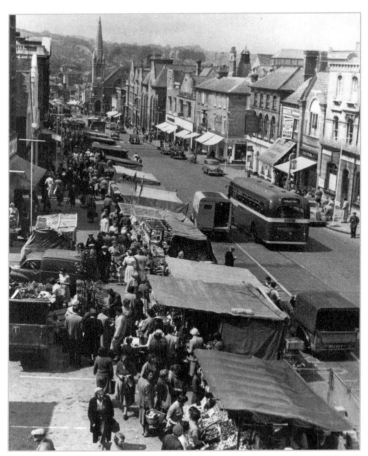

The fruit and veg market is in full swing in this 1950s view of North Street.

Looking down North Street with the spire of the Methodist church clearly visible. Note the tree growing on Harvey's roof garden, to the left.

from London, who wanted to sell clothes and general household goods in North Street. The borough eventually permitted this and by the 1930s North Street market on Saturday nights was a lively place indeed, packed with street sellers and their entertaining sales patter.

By the 1950s it was back to daytime markets on Fridays and Saturdays with only fruit, vegetables and flowers sold. However, in 1979, under pressure from the North Street Market Traders' Association, permission was again granted to traders who sold other types of goods to be allowed pitches.

Of some of the other shops that once occupied North Street, there was Milletts, that specialised in army surplus wear. Next door was the Surrey Arms pub – the local for staff on the *Surrey Advertiser* just around the corner in Martyr Road. Pascalls had its pram shop at number 13, and further on down was the Guildford Theatre, and next to it the Guildford & District Co-op's store. There was also Jarman's the tobacconist and W. Pullen & Sons, florists.

Beyond the junction with Woodbridge Road and the Methodist church was the Guildford Radio and Television Company, outfitters H.A. Newell & Sons, grocers Hall's Stores, childrenswear specialists Bon Marché and another outfitters, Shirley Bros.

Alfred Bull & Co. marquee contractors, was based where the library is today.

Going up the south side were even more shops (and pubs), now long gone, but which will be remembered by many. As well as the Little White Lion, there was the Lion & Crown Hotel, plus the Vintners Arms. George's fishmongers was on the corner of Swan Lane, then Bernard's the butchers, Burnett's boot repairers and jewellers W.J. Bayne. Further along was The Chocolate Shop, Chas Chaplin the newsagent, Withey's the fishmonger, plus other businesses including Drewetts photographers, milliners Furlong, butchers and grocers Robert Wasley Ltd, Jones the newsagents and the stationers and confectioners Lavells Ltd.

Gammons was situated on the corner of North Street and Market Street. The shop was a large drapery store and the Gammon family were not only respected traders in the town but did much for the welfare of Guildfordians and the churches in general.

The founder, J.F. Gammon, who died in 1916, did much to help the Salvation Army in its early

Looking up Market Street from North Street with Gammons store on the left and Lavells on the right. Note the sign for the Wimpy Bar.

The Dolphin pub on the corner of North Street and Chertsey Street. The building that replaced it was occupied by the furnishing store Habitat. It is now TGI Friday's restaurant and also the studios and offices of 96.4 The Eagle radio station.

days in Guildford. The Salvation Army suffered a great deal of resentment and even violence at one time within the borough. Mr Gammon presented a petition to the then mayor, William Trigg, requesting that it received police protection. However, this had little effect until the Home Secretary took remedial action by way of a special messenger to call on the Mayor and present an ultimatum.

Further on up North Street and around the corner, next to the junction with the High Street, is Central Buildings. This was once the offices of Cow & Gate. The dairy firm was run by the Gates family, whose forebears had been grocers in Guildford since 1771. Their West Surrey Central Dairy Company took off in the latter years of the 19th century and the name was later changed to Cow & Gate. The shop in the High Street, next to Abbot's Hospital, was not large enough from which to run the rapidly expanding business, so it moved its offices to the Central Buildings in the 1920s. Its milk delivery branch, Home Counties Dairies, had its headquarters in Cross Lanes, off Epsom Road. Cow & Gate merged with United Dairies in 1959 to form Unigate.

CHAPTER SIX

GUILDFORD PEOPLE

John Brownrigg

Perhaps one of the most talented architects to work from Guildford was John Brownrigg.

Built on a slender budget and occupying a very small site next to the River Wey, is his Yvonne Arnaud Theatre. Despite its actual size the building has the feeling of a much larger theatre.

John Brownrigg had many revolutionary planning ideas which were well ahead of their time. He certainly did not find favour with some of the planners and councillors of the day, who did not welcome spending large sums of money on public buildings.

However, John Brownrigg believed that anything in building terms could be achieved, but it would, of course, cost money. He went on record to state that Tunsgate Arch was a fine gateway but led to nowhere in particular. He believed the arch would lend itself to a fine processional way from the Guildhall up to South Hill, on which the cathedral should have been built. He also advocated a ski-lift system from outlying car parks to the town centre.

His 'temporary' parade of shops on the west side of the upper High Street, from what had been Masseys chemists to Allen House, has stood the test of time. At the end, which now adjoins the grounds of the Royal Grammar School, he placed a plinth for a piece of artwork. To this day it has never been used.

His father, Annesley, had been an architect and had set up an office in Haslemere in 1910. His work was mainly residential.

In the 1930s John studied at the Bartlett School of Architecture, qualifying in 1936. He began working

The architect of the Yvonne Arnaud Theatre, John Brownrigg (far left), with the theatre's first director-administrator, Laurier Lister, and Hugh McLellan, on the board of directors and husband of the late Yvonne Arnaud.

Seen on the right is the row of shops and offices in the upper High Street that was by John Brownrigg.

on his own until he joined the Royal Navy during World War Two.

He served on the *Ark Royal* as a torpedo officer. He was on the ship when it was itself torpedoed in the Mediterranean in 1941. John managed to get into a lifeboat, but after a while went back to the ship to retrieve his Box Brownie camera. He then took a picture of the stricken ship, which he sent to the *Daily Mirror,* who printed the picture on its front page.

The result was that all hell broke loose and he found himself in considerable trouble. The picture was released without the permission of the censor!

John never got over the loss of his shipmate, Able Seaman Mitchell, the only sailor to die when the *Ark Royal* was sunk. He wrote a poem about him that was included in a book of his verse, published after his death in 2003 by Claude Kauffmann, the chairman of the County Club, of which John had been a valued member.

An Epitaph For Able Seaman Mitchell

It must be lonely, Mitch,
Down there below,
As you, still keep that long watch,
Started 50 years ago.

With only silent squid and curious eels for company,
Hang that great ship yet,
Between the sea's ceiling and the ocean floor,
Buoyed up by air entrapped.

In that great hull,
Alternatively, has she found a final resting place,
Softly settled on the bed,
Of the enfolding waves,
Where once ranged and ruled.

In power and dignity,
Although in life, your part was small,
In death, you play a more important role,
As proud custodian in sole command.

After the war, John Brownrigg went on a refresher course at the Architectural Association, where he met Newman Turner and Stephen Cruickshank. The three of them set up the practice of Brownrigg & Turner, based at Bramley Mill.

In the late 1950s, the firm merged with the company that John's father had set up, to create Duncan Scott Brownrigg & Turner, with offices at 41–42 Parliament Street in London. Meanwhile, the Guildford practice of Brownrigg & Turner continued.

John's main interest was in residential work. Eric Ambrose, the architectural correspondent of the *Ideal Home* magazine, often featured John's work in the magazine. Many prospective clients contacted John through that particular publication. One such commission that came his way was for a house in Hampstead, of which the main feature was a staircase that arrived on the ground floor in the centre of a pond. Stepping stones were used to reach the main body of the hall.

The house John designed for racing driver Stirling Moss had one of the first sets of electronically controlled garage doors and a remote-controlled television system.

John was interested in new ways and methods of building homes and the materials used in their construction. He was instrumental in the research and development of timber-framed prefabricated houses designed for the Guildford-based firm Guildway.

He designed his own home, set in a disused quarry in Guildford. His studio, which looked into the wonderful amphitheatre of the overgrown quarry, became a haven for him in his retirement as he took up the art of silversmithing.

John took great delight in encouraging young people in arts and crafts. His inherent wit and optimism made him a natural and energetic teacher, right up until his death.

Remembering those who died for king and country

In a quiet corner of Holy Trinity Church in the High Street is a small marble memorial bearing the names of 11 young Guildfordians who lost their lives during World War One. They had been proud members of the 9th Guildford Scouts.

At the foot of the tablet is the symbol of a point within a circle indicating that they have gone to their eternal home after paying the supreme sacrifice in the names of both king and country.

This memorial was originally unveiled in the Old Congregational Chapel in Chapel Street on 16 October 1919, by a General Ellis.

The plaque in Holy Trinity Church commemorating former members of the 9th Guildford Scout Troop who died in World War One.

Reg Streeter grew up in Stoughton and went to Northmead Boys' School. He worked as a plumber with Maynard & Mulley, based in Church Road, but was best known as a local amateur boxer. He was a member of the Onslow Boxing Club under the tuition of Pat Keens. He fought bouts at the Sandfield Terrace Drill Hall and also joined the Guildford Air Training Corps 261 Squadron. By being a member of the latter he would have been entitled to join the RAF when he was called to do his National Service. However, he joined the army instead. At the time some people said Reg did this as he believed he would get more time to pursue boxing, although that holds little truth as all the services encouraged sports.

Soon after his death, the press tracked down the Streeter family and his mother bravely gave some interviews. In one daily newspaper she said that in his last letter home he had written: 'Mum, I am scared. We are all prepared to do our duty and die if necessary.' She added that she had received dozens of letters from all over the country from people offering their sympathy.

Men from the Queen's Regiment who died during the Malaya conflict are commemorated on this plaque in Holy Trinity Church.

Alderman Vic Tidy

Alderman Vic Tidy at his home in Old Palace Road.

Alderman H.V. Tidy was a man you could pass in the street without giving a second glance. Modest yes, but few ever knew that he was awarded the Military Medal during World War One, rising to the rank of sergeant-major.

His aim in life was freedom and justice for all, especially those he represented in Guildford's Westborough ward. To his friends, this Labour councillor always preferred to be known as Vic.

However, he was not so well received by some of his more snobbish fellow councillors, who believed those who served on the council should not live in a council house. Vic Tidy did, of course, live in a council house, in Old Palace Road.

In Vic Tidy's time, the more affluent tended to regard council house occupants as second class. And worse still, an expense to be paid for by the rate-payers.

It did not go down well with other councillors that Vic Tidy worked in the back shop area of the Co-op. Some said, quite unkindly, that he was just a floor sweeper.

Born in Drummond Road in 1897, he went to Stoke School and joined the Boy Scouts in 1906. He became the first King's Scout in Guildford and at the outbreak of World War One was a senior scout attached to the Queen's Royal West Surrey Regiment at Stoughton Barracks as a messenger boy.

He travelled to and from France with the British Expeditionary Force on three occasions. He enlisted in the Queen's in June 1915, returned to France and was wounded. After recovering in a Cardiff hospital he returned to the battle front, being transferred to the Royal Welch Regiment in August 1916.

After the war he joined the printing trade, working for both Billings and Biddles in Guildford. In his spare time he promoted dances and social events in the town, particularly at the old Borough Hall.

During World War Two Vic Tidy went to work for the Guildford and District Co-operative Society and became a trade union official. He joined the Labour Party and became chairman of his local branch. He served as a sergeant in the Stag Hill company of the Home Guard and in 1945 he joined the council representing Onslow ward. He lost his seat in 1948, but was elected for the Westborough ward in 1950.

In honour of his services to the council, he was made an alderman in April 1962, on the resignation of Alderman Arthur Williams. However, he contested his seat in the borough elections a month later as he had already been nominated. Strictly, if voted back in, as an alderman he could not take his place on the council. But if he had stepped down from the election fight, it would have been a two-way battle between a Tory and a communist. Vic knew that the seat should go to a Labour councillor. So he stood and won the seat. There was then, of course, a vacancy on the council, and so a by-election had to be arranged at a later date.

There was a good deal of controversy over Alderman Tidy's proposals for a new route for the Guildford A3 bypass. However, if he had been taken more seriously, the often-seen bottleneck on the A3 as it passes beside Westborough and the Guildford Business Park (the former Dennis works), would not occur.

He backed the plan for a new road that would leave the A3 at Burpham and cut across open country in the direction of the then Women's Royal Army Camp (now Queen Elizabeth Park), across common land around Rydes Hill and on past the current Royal Surrey County Hospital, to rejoin the A3 at its junction with the A31.

It's most unlikely that such a plan would find any supporters today, but several decades ago it was a viable scheme that if built would have made travelling in and around Guildford very different. Even when the plan for the current A3 bypass (from the Stoke interchange to near what is called the 'Dennis roundabout') was finalised, Alderman Tidy warned that this was in no way a long-term solution. He was also a member of the Guildford Road Safety Committee, from 1947 to 1967, and was its chairman for 13 years.

Alderman Tidy gave a good deal to the town and also to his beloved Guildford City Football Club, of which he was the chairman of its supporters' club for 25 years, and also a director of the club.

Vic Tidy's sudden death, at the age of 75 in September 1972, came as a shock to many. The *Surrey Advertiser* noted that he was 'a man who fought many battles on Guildford's behalf, his forthright and down-to-earth oratory in the council chamber caused its members to stir more than once, in the past'.

William Harvey OBE

There was a great sense of loss when Alderman William Harvey OBE died in November 1946 at the age of 62. He had given more than 20 years' service to Guildford and had put it on the international map with his work fund scheme that raised money and gave jobs to local men in the depression of the 1930s.

For this he was made a freeman of the borough. He was mayor for three years and his ladies' wear shop was an established business in the town. The shop outlived him and, still bearing his name, became a large department store.

William Harvey was born in Ashford, Kent, in 1883, and educated at Bethany House School, Goudhurst, and University College, Folkestone.

After working in London stores, including Marshall & Snelgrove, Derry & Toms and Peter Robinson, he came to Guildford in 1911 to work for Cable, Reeks & Co. in the High Street. He enlisted in 1916 and saw active service in France during World War One as a motorcycle despatch rider attached to the Royal Artillery. For his gallantry he was awarded the Military Medal.

Alderman William Harvey OBE, pictured when he was Mayor of Guildford.

William Harvey's drapery store was originally in the Playhouse Arcade. It later transferred to the High Street, as seen here in the mid–1950s.

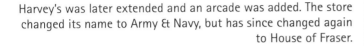

Harvey's was later extended and an arcade was added. The store changed its name to Army & Navy, but has since changed again to House of Fraser.

In 1918, he acquired the drapery business of John Reeks, and in 1922, when the Playhouse Arcade opened, moved his business there. His shop ran the entire length of one side of the arcade.

In the year of his death the business became a limited company and later moved to premises on the High Street. Here it traded as Harvey's of Guildford. An arcade was opened that ran down to North Street. In the 1970s the Harvey's name finally disappeared when the store was renamed Army & Navy. That name has now gone, as today it is House of Fraser. The premises underwent a massive rebuild a few years ago.

William Harvey was elected as a councillor for the Stoke ward in 1926. His first chairmanship was of the public grounds committee. A keen gardener himself, he was instrumental in the development of Stoke Park as a leisure amenity, particularly the rose garden. He was also the founder and a president of the Guildford Rose Society.

He was made mayor in 1931 and at once strived to develop a social conscience for Guildford. The Guildford Council of Social Service met in a room at his home in Stoke Road. Unemployment was rising and William Harvey knew he had to help those who were out of work. At the time he said: 'I want to do something more for these fellows than give away pounds of tea at Christmas.' He formed a small group who came up with the Guildford Work Fund Scheme. It was brilliantly simple. Guildfordians who were earning a wage, or suitably well off, were asked to contribute to it. It was launched when he was re-elected as mayor in November 1932. The council had set aside £3,000 to pay men for much-needed work in the borough and generous contributions from the townsfolk brought in another £7,700. That may not seem much by today's standard of wages, but it was a sum back then that provided 150,490 hours of work.

The fund calculated that by estimating the total number of unemployed people in the borough, each man given a job through the fund would receive a minimum of 35 shillings a week for about 35 hours' work.

Local firms, churches, the Rotary Club and the Guildford branch of the Royal British Legion helped with the fundraising, of which there were many events. Jobs that were found for the men ranged from weeding the sports ground, planting hedges, removing chalk from the caverns in Racks Close and, without doubt, the biggest project of all, the building of the lido.

More than 8,000 people packed the grounds of the new open-air swimming pool on 21 June 1933 to see William Harvey officially open it by diving in. The news story and that of the work fund went around the world.

In the New Years' Honours list of 1933 he was appointed an Officer of the British Empire, for services to relief and unemployment, and in March 1934 the town council made him an honorary freeman of the borough.

He was involved in a number of other local projects that included what was the forerunner of the town's citizens advice bureau, a clothing depot, the Personal Service League, Sunday evening concerts, a programme of lectures, an allotments and seeds scheme, while also being the chairman of the town's Electricity Committee.

Furthermore, he sat on many committees. He was a governor of the Royal Grammar School, president of the Guildford & District Boy Scouts' Association, a governor of Abbot's Hospital, administrative trustee of the Poyle Charity, a member of the Food Committee and of the Guildford Gardeners' Association.

During World War Two, although then suffering from ill-heath, he insisted on undertaking fire-watching duties and was in charge of ARP in Merrow.

He was a keen cyclist, but in his later years he appeared to hide his illness from all but his closest friends. He died of a heart attack while at the home of his son-in-law, Gerald Wilson, who himself at the time was the town clerk.

The Mayor of Guildford at the time of William Harvey's death was Councillor A.W. Graham Brown. Paying tribute, Mr Graham Brown said: 'He seemed to occupy a position detached from the uneasy buffeting and divisions of political conflict, always seeking only to preserve the antiquity and beauty of the town.

'He was a man with deep religious convictions, a religion that, simple and real, was expressed in the habits of his daily life of which he said little, but kept resolutely.'

Alderman Lawrence Powell, who was made a freeman of the borough of Guildford. The portrait was painted by William E. Narraway.

Alderman Lawrence Powell

The greatest honour that Guildford can bestow on any person is that of freeman, which among its more bizarre privileges grants permission to drive sheep over the Town Bridge. The honour is not given lightly, but is according to outstanding merit and service. Two generations of one Guildford family have had this honour.

Thomas Wilde Powell of Piccards Rough was the first such freeman of the borough of Guildford, appointed in 1897. He was also the first chairman of the Royal Grammar School after the school's 'reconstruction' in 1890. His son, Alderman Herbert Powell, also served as chairman of the school's governors, as did his son Lawrence.

Lawrence Powell more than deserved his own appointment as freeman, as he played a very positive part in forming the town as it is known today.

He was made mayor in 1935, the same year in which Sir John Jarvis was elected as Guildford's MP, when Onslow Village Ltd gave 50 acres of land from Mount Farm to Compton Corner as a public open space, and when the Diocesan Conference decided to go ahead to build the first portion of the cathedral on Stag Hill.

Alderman Powell played an important part in the birth of the new cathedral. This included raising funds for one of the great bronze doors on the south side of the transept. It depicts the elemental occupations of men. The other door was funded by a Miss Courtauld, who lived in Seale. That door portrays the corresponding basic tasks of women.

Other notable events in 1936, while he was still Mayor, included the laying of the foundation stone for the cathedral, the opening of the Jarvis Maternity Home in Stoughton Road, and the purchase for £28,000 of the Chantries as a permanent open space.

He oversaw the reopening of the former corn exchange market, now Tunsgate, for vehicles to pass through, by the repositioning of two of its pillars.

Following the outbreak of the Spanish Civil War, Alderman Powell launched a fund to bring 40 Basque refugee children to Guildford. They were cared for at Ardmore House in Stoughton.

He witnessed the laying of the foundation stone of the West Surrey Technical College at Stoke Park, by the then chairman of Surrey County Council, Sir Philip Henriques, and in 1937, Lawrence Powell opened the fire station on Ladymead.

Alderman Powell presided over the sale of Guildford Cottages Ltd, at the company's annual meeting held at his family home at Weir House, Millmead, in 1955. For more than 20 years the business owned eight houses. The borough council agreed to take on the task and paid £2,000 for the privilege.

He later gifted the historic Weir House to the National Trust. For a time he continued to live there until moving to Rivermead in Flower Walk. He described Weir House as a Regency residence built some time between Trafalgar and Waterloo!

His love of music led him to commission the composer Geoffrey

Weir House, Millmead, the home of Alderman Laurence Powell, seen here in about 1950.

Bush to write a Guildford symphony. It was heard in 1957 at the time of the 700th anniversary of the town's first recorded charter. The work was played by the Guildford Municipal Orchestra conducted by Crossley Clitheroe. Alderman Powell went on to become the president of The Guildford Musical Society later that year.

The welfare of the young was another topic that interested him. He served for 22 years on the Surrey Education Committee. In total, he served on more than 50 town committees and in 1960, he became a justice of the peace on the Guildford borough bench.

One of the more unique ideas floated by Lawrence Powell began with him pointing out that the ancient Greek word for 'town' was very similar to that of 'civilisation'. He remarked that in Europe the 'towns' of Florence, Sienna, and Venice compete against each other in 'civilisation'. He suggested that it would be a good thing if Guildford, Winchester, Lewes and Chichester staged a grand competition every 10 years to be judged on such things as public buildings, street cleaning, railway stations, shop windows, the arts, and so on. He believed that such a competition would concentrate the mind and also stimulate the use of the ballot box.

Alderman Lawrence Powell died at St Luke's Hospital in 1973 at the age of 84.

The Revd Roy Trevivian

The Revd Roy Trevivian may only have been a priest in the parish of Westborough for seven and a half years, but this well-liked, charismatic and outspoken man – on behalf of those less well off, is still remembered by many.

The Revd Roy Trevivian (right) mixes cement with John 'Geordie' Brown during the building of the church-cum-hall at Park Barn in 1964.

He inspired the people of Park Barn to build their own church-cum-hall and went on a bricklaying course at Guildford Technical College so that he could help them with the work. He was central to the incident when the then Bishop of Guildford, the Rt Revd George Reindorp, was photographed doing the twist at a fundraising event, and received a hail of criticism after the picture appeared in newspapers and magazines around the world.

Born in Manchester in 1921, Roy Trevivian served with the RAF in World War Two. He then trained for the Methodist ministry at Richmond College, London University, but his career as a minister with the Methodists was shortlived. He disliked its system of using ministers to pastor half a dozen scattered congregations and the wasted energy spent travelling long distances on his 125cc BSA motorcycle. In 1949, in frustration, he resigned. He was soon to receive an offer from an old cricketing friend, the then Bishop of Guildford, the Rt Revd Dr Henry Montgomerie Campbell, who offered to ordain him into the Church of England. He trained for the Anglican priesthood at Lichfield Theological College and came to St Francis' Church in Beckingham Road, Westborough, Guildford, in October 1956 after serving as curate in the parish of St Mary the Virgin, Burgh Heath, Epsom.

Roy Trevivian was 35 years old when he came to Guildford with his wife Yvonne. He had strong socialist principles and a crusading zeal. He drove around the parish of Westborough in a black Morris 8 car.

In March 1959, while speaking to those gathered for a church conference at Holy Trinity Cathedral Church, Roy Trevivian criticised part of Guildford council's housing policy as thoroughly un-Christian. He called on the council to reconsider its methods of funding the building of flats for old people. A couple of months earlier, the council had decided to increase council house rents by two shillings a week.

As Park Barn was being developed, a piece of land at the junction of Southway, Applegarth Avenue and Cabell Road was set aside for the building of a church. In 1960, Roy Trevivian persuaded the Diocese of Guildford to buy the land and then struck a bargain with local residents. He told them that if they would supply the labour to build the church, he would see that the necessary funds were raised.

The *Surrey Advertiser* of 16 September 1961 noted: 'There is no good standing around trying to look heavenly when there is an earthly job to be done. That is the belief of the Revd Roy Trevivian, Vicar of Westborough, and his curate, the Revd Paul Barber. Both have just signed on for the bricklayers' practical course at Guildford Technical College.

'The reason? Both wish to be able to take their place alongside the tradesmen of the parish who have volunteered their services to build a church-cum-hall on the Park Barn estate.

'Mr Trevivian said: "If those men are going to give their time to help us we should be willing to give some of our time to them. We hope to have acquired enough skill to do our own work, indeed up to a standard by which the bricklayers' union would be pleased to receive us as honorary members".'

Seventy people signed on to help, with Ray Perfett, a building foreman by trade, and who lived just three doors away from the church site, agreeing to supervise the whole operation. In total about 120 people worked on the building project over the following four years until the church was consecrated in May 1965.

The *Surrey Advertiser* of 28 March 1962 ran a story and photograph showing the foundations being dug. A couple of years later Roy Trevivian recalled: 'Between 30 and 40 men and women dug and trundled away barrows of solid clay.'

He recalled that heavy rain then threatened to ruin all their good work. He said: 'We couldn't afford wood to shore up the trenches and the sides crumbled. We dug them out again – while it rained. Morale was sinking fast as they caved in a second time. Paul (Barber) and I spent two days, without hardly a break, wading in mud and water, bailing out with buckets. Trenches that were 4ft 6in wide increased to 6ft.

The midweek *Surrey Advertiser* of 23 March 1962 ran a story and a picture of the digging of the foundations for the church-cum-hall in Park Barn. The Revd Roy Trevivian is pictured in the centre, wielding a spade.

'The third time we dug them the sides held and the weather improved just long enough for us to get the foundation concrete in.'

The foundations and brickwork, up to the damp-proof course, were complete by 28 May 1962. By 23 July of that year, work on the concrete floor and the drains had been finished.

The hot summer of 1962 proved to be an eventful one. It was a lovely warm evening on 10 August, and a parish barbecue was held on the now completed floor of the church-cum-hall. The event was a thank you to the people who had been working so hard on the project. The then Bishop of Guildford, the Rt Revd George Reindorp, was the special guest. He certainly got into the swing of things and was photographed in the *Surrey Advertiser* on 18 August dancing the twist with a Mrs Pat MacDonell. Soon the picture had been circulated around the world. A Russian newspaper described him as 'the decadent bishop', while an Australian magazine called him 'a rock 'n' roller'. It was later reported that the photograph was on display in an anti-Christian museum in Moscow!

Roy Trevivian used the columns of the *Surrey Advertiser* to defend the bishop's fancy footwork. However, there followed a number of letters of criticism to the newspaper and directly to Mr Trevivian himself. Some of the correspondence was quite hostile and abusive. On the other hand, others endorsed Mr Trevivian for backing the bishop's harmless antics and joining in the fun.

Work on the building slowed somewhat due to the cold winter of 1963. But by January 1964, the roof had been finished and the glass fitted into the windows. A film crew from ATV came to the nearly completed church-cum-hall and broadcast a communion service live on Palm Sunday, 1964.

Roy Trevivian was certainly wise to the power of the media in portraying Christianity, and it was perhaps not a total surprise when, in August 1964, he announced that he would be leaving the parish of Westborough and Guildford to take up a post with the BBC as a producer of religious radio programmes.

St Francis' Church was packed for Roy Trevivian's final service, held there on 5 October 1964. In his sermon, he preached that following the teachings of Jesus Christ means caring about people in need. He also told the congregation: 'It means we should adopt a special way of dealing with our enemies – not the Old Testament way of an eye for an eye and a tooth for a tooth.' However, speaking of his enemies, who he tried not to be bitter about, he said: 'As you know I enjoy a good fight. But I always find that if my opponents are fighting from their integrity, then my faith holds and doesn't destroy.'

The Revd Walter Boulton

The Revd Walter Boulton was an outspoken clergyman and his criticism of the borough council's housing and roads policy almost certainly cost him the position of Dean of Guildford Cathedral.

He was appointed Rector of Holy Trinity and St Mary's Church in 1952. The appointment also bestowed upon him the title of Provost of Holy Trinity. At the time it was the Cathedral Church of the Diocese of Guildford, while the new cathedral was being built at Stag Hill.

Previously, the Revd Boulton had ministered in India for 20 years where, after a controversial sermon in Calcutta Cathedral, traders raised a petition asking for his expulsion. He came to Guildford via a church in Fleet, Hampshire, where he had served for four years.

Walter Boulton was a warm sincere man, much loved by those who really knew him.

The post of provost was one that would, at the time of the consecration of the new cathedral, be replaced by that of the Dean. It was therefore a great shock that in the run-up to the consecration of the Cathedral Church of the Holy Spirit in 1961, the Crown did not grant Walter Boulton that title.

The Revd Walter Boulton, who was Provost of Guildford Cathedral.

Unfortunately, the ceremony could not go ahead without someone at least acting the part of the Dean, so the Revd Boulton, as provost, was asked to step in for the day.

It was a poignant moment on the eve of the consecration, when, standing on the steps of the chancel, he was interviewed on television by Richard Dimbleby about the unusual situation he was in, playing the part of the Dean when he was not supposed to do so.

The consecration of the cathedral was thus clouded by the bitter argument which followed. In a very short time a petition containing more than 2,000 signatures was raised and sent to the Queen. So strong was this swell of discontent that the then Archbishop of Canterbury, Dr Geoffrey Fisher, tried to cool the atmosphere by the unusual step of issuing a statement supporting the Crown's advisors. He stated that the Revd Boulton had been an inspiring, loving and successful pastor and leader, but that other gifts were also needed for the whole range of demands which are presented by a new cathedral. He went on to state that a right place should be made for Walter Boulton, who was was then found a position as rector of the East Midlands parish of Market Overton with Thistleton, in Rutland. He retired to Sussex in 1971.

The Revd Boulton's coup de grâce, so to speak, had been delivered with resounding effect at the civic service of 1958. His words 'big brother bureaucracy', aimed towards the town's roads policy, and 'monstrosities' of the High Street, were flung at his captive audience – the borough's councillors, who were sitting uneasily a few yards from his pulpit.

He returned to preach at Holy Trinity on just one occasion, but to a packed congregation. This was in 1963, during the service to commemorate the 200th anniversary of the rebuilding of the church. He died in 1984, aged 83.

CHAPTER SEVEN

HITTING THE HEADLINES

Rail crash

One man later died and several people were injured at Guildford railway station on 18 September 1953 when the 3.12pm train from Waterloo crashed through the buffers at platform one, ploughing into the stationmaster's office.

As the train approached the station from the Cobham line, its driver, motorman William Sherman, began to apply the brakes, but to his horror they failed and the 300-ton electric train crashed through the rough safety area known as 'the drag and hit'.

With its bogey wheels torn off, the train smashed into an office building. Inside were the stationmaster, Mr F. Selby; inspector Arthur Saunders; Leslie Barrett, a relief assistant stationmaster; Leonard Brewster; Ernest Turner and Josephine Matthews.

Mrs Matthews, who lived in Grange Road, escaped through the office door at the last moment before the impact, but suffered severe shock and was taken to hospital. The others were trapped under a pile of bricks and splintered wood.

Taxi drivers from the rank outside the station quickly forced their way into the wrecked office and immediately assisted in the rescue. The train driver, along with four passengers, jumped to safety before the impact and escaped injury.

The Royal Surrey County Hospital in Farnham Road turned its out-patients ward into an emergency ward to receive the injured. It was reported at the time that this was done with the precision of a military operation. The talk at the scene was that it was a miracle that no one had been killed, but this was a little premature, as unfortunately the relief assistant stationmaster later died of his injuries.

The leading coach of the 3.12pm from Waterloo embedded in the stationmaster's office at Guildford in 1953.

Damaged coaches after the crash.

At the inquest into the crash, the *Surrey Advertiser* reported that the jury exonerated the train driver as he did all he could have done to avoid the accident. Knowing that there was a problem with the electro-pneumatic brakes and a delay before the train's other brakes, the Westinghouse System, would apply themselves, the driver attempted to put the train's motors into reverse.

The newspaper noted that a similar, but lesser, accident had occurred at the platform earlier in May of that year, but no one had been injured.

The Queen's visit in 1957

'The borough will treasure this June day,' reported the *Surrey Advertiser* in its edition of 29 June 1957. It was the occasion of a visit two days earlier by the Queen and the Duke of Edinburgh that marked the 700th anniversary of Guildford receiving its first royal charter by Henry III.

It certainly was a day to remember. It was the first time in 300 years that a reigning monarch had visited the borough, and, as tradition demanded, she was presented with a plum cake as a token of affection – a tradition that goes back to mediaeval times.

Children present bricks to the Queen on her visit to Guildford Cathedral in 1957.

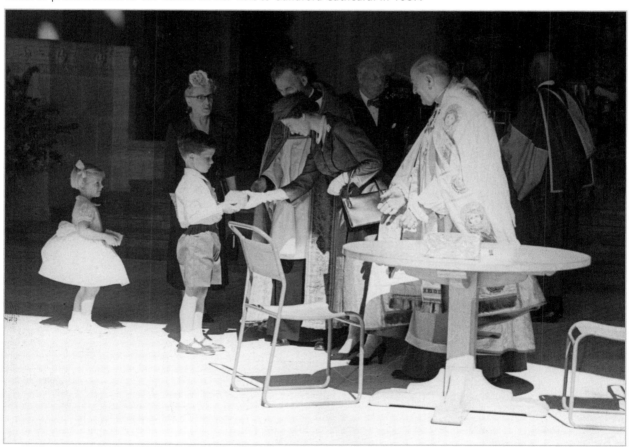

The Queen with the then Bishop of Guildford, the Rt Revd Ivor Watkins, outside Guildford Cathedral.

A huge crowd was at the cathedral to see the Queen.

Brian Holt was an apprentice baker with Ayers. With the firm's managing director, William Hambrook, Brian helped bake the plum cake that was presented to the Queen during her visit.

Unfortunately, no one was sure which ingredients to use. Master baker William Hambrook of Ayres bakery was given the task to to come up with the solution. A recipe dating back to 1700 was found, but he finally settled on one dating from the 19th century.

The weather was perfect for the royal visit. A full six hours before the Queen was due to arrive, a woman in her seventies was the first spectator to stake her pitch outside the Guildhall in the High Street, with a stool and a packed lunch.

Children who were patients at St Luke's Hospital gathered in York Road to watch the royals pass, while residents of Abbot's Hospital, resplendent in their formal gowns, stood in the upper High Street. The *Surrey Advertiser* reported that one of those from Abbot's Hospital waxed lyrical about the time he'd gone to London to see Queen Victoria's diamond jubilee parade in 1897.

In Guildford, the Queen and her party were officially received by a large number of notable townspeople, including the then recorder, Mr T. Christmas Humphrey.

In her speech inside the Guildhall, the Queen drew a link between Guildford and Windsor Castles, saying that 700 years ago they were only separated by a great forest, the antiquity of which stretched back to the time of William the Conqueror. She likened Guildford's then unfinished cathedral at Stag Hill to the cross on the royal orb.

From the Guildhall, the royal party made its way to the cathedral, which at the time only consisted of the nave and its crossing. There, the

The cover of a leaflet promoting the Pageant of Guildford that took place at Shalford Park from 26 June to 6 July 1957. Ticket prices ranged from £1 1s to 2s 6d. The leaflet stated that '1,000 performers will bring to life the town's history in a swift-moving spectacle, in which the modern techniques of stage-craft, light and sound, will serve 700 years of history'.

Queen was greeted by the then Bishop of Guildford, the Rt Revd Ivor Watkins.

The cathedral's architect, Sir Edward Maufe, was introduced, as was the formidable fundraiser Eleonora Iredale. Many other people connected with the work of the diocese and the building of the cathedral also had the chance to meet the royal party.

Then it was on to the Royal Surrey County Hospital for a quick visit, before reaching the Sports Ground in Woodbridge Road, where the royal party arrived too late to see the end of the match between Surrey and Hampshire. Surrey had won, and their captain, Peter May, apologised to the Queen for the early finish. He said that he had not wanted the match prolonged in case it rained.

A 20-overs match was arranged, during which a player hit a six right into the Mayor's tea tent. According to the newspaper report, the ball was smartly fielded by a waitress!

Perhaps the highlight of the day was the Pageant of Guildford that was held at Shalford Park and directed by Christopher Ede. The production designer was David Clarke, who went on to be a successful pageant master himself.

The park had been prepared the autumn before with the planting of trees, which formed a backdrop for the cast of more than 800 players. The show started with Guildford being granted its royal charter and followed a path through history up to the 20th century, with a portrayal of Lord Baden Powell and the town's very own Queen's Regiment. Both Baden Powell and the regiment had been honoured with the freedom of the borough.

The finale showed a symbol of faith in the future with a small family walking towards a floodlit mock-up of the completed Cathedral Church of the Holy Spirit. The pageant ran for several nights and on the last night the 4,000-strong audience rose spontaneously to join in the singing of the popular old hymn, *O Lord Our Help In Ages Past*.

The pageant in Shalford Park in 1957.

Firefighters at work the morning after a fire had swept through Guildford's repertory theatre in 1963.

Guildford Theatre fire

The Guildford Theatre in North Street had staged many dramas, but perhaps none more dramatic than its last performance during the early hours of hours of Wednesday 10 April 1963.

Local residents were woken by a resounding explosion just before dawn and by breakfast time the theatre stage and auditorium had been reduced to a smouldering shell. However, the dressing rooms and offices were largely unaffected.

It was reported that lumps of red-hot charcoal, the size of eggs, were thrown into the air with great force. In tackling the blaze, firefighters rescued the occupants of a flat next door.

In reporting the fire, the *Surrey Advertiser* of 13 April stated that 'flames and sparks shot into the sky as half a dozen appliances brought hoses to bear, watched by a small crowd of people in the dawn light'.

Eyewitness Eileen Emmings, who lived in an adjoining flat, told the newspaper's reporter that the heat from the flames was terrific and could be felt standing at the flat window.

There was also a lot of damage to the neighbouring Co-op's premises on the Leapale Road side of the site. The second floor was completely gutted and the entire stock of bedding lost. Stocks of carpet and lino also had to be written off.

However, damage at the Haydon Place end of the building was only slight and the store was soon open for business as best it could.

Another eyewitness, Haydon Place newsagent and greengrocer, Mr G. Langhorn, was one of the first on the scene. He was woken by a large explosion and, pausing only long enough to put on a pair of trousers, he ran towards North Street. He told the newspaper: 'The roof was well alight by then.' He also said that to begin with the wind was blowing down Haydon Place, carrying the flames and burning embers in that direction. Suddenly it veered in the opposite direction, and Mr Langhorn added: 'I am sure that the change in wind direction saved the fire from spreading to houses in Haydon Place.'

Once the fire had been put out, the general manager of the theatre, Eric Longworth, was soon on the scene organising its salvage operation. Some years later he returned to acting and played the part of the town clerk in the classic TV comedy *Dad's Army*.

The fire occurred at the time when the Co-op, which owned the whole site, had given notice to the theatre management that it required the building space for a new food store. The takeover date was planned for the autumn of 1963.

However, plans were well under way to build a new theatre on a river island site beside the former Town Mill. The then princely sum of £125,000 had been raised and from its campaign office in the old police station, opposite the site of the fire, the new theatre appeal committee was still raising cash.

The popular French-born actress, Yvonne Arnaud, who lived with her husband Hugh McLellan in

This part of the building was completely destroyed in the blaze.

Guildford, had died just a few years before. They had been members of the voluntary board of directors of the Guildford Theatre, and so it was agreed that the new theatre should bear her name. It opened in 1965.

The Guildford Theatre had been formed in 1946 by the theatrical champions Patrick Henderson and Roger Winton. The North Street site had previously been the Borough Hall and assize court. The former Theatre Royal had also been there. The Theatre Royal's demise in 1933, due to the popularity of cinema, was a great loss to local theatre-goers. They then had to travel to the Hippodrome at Aldershot for their live variety entertainment until the Guildford Theatre opened.

The loss of the Borough Hall, a fine structure of local Bargate stone, was also mourned. But at the time of the fire, its replacement, the civic hall, had been open for about a year.

In 1924, the assize court had been a 'stage' for a notorious murder trial. Frenchman Jean Pierre Vaquier had been accused of using strychnine to poison Alfred George Poynter Jones, the publican of the Blue Anchor pub at Byfleet, after an alleged affair with the publican's wife. Unfortunately, for the Frenchman, the English court did not recognise his plea of a crime of passion, and to his great dismay he finished up on the gallows. It is claimed that he made quite a spectacle of himself in the dock, posturing and preening his way though the trial in the certain belief that he would be acquitted.

The room the assize court was held in was used for other purposes and functions as the judges only sat at certain times of the year.

A strong protest was made by one assize judge when he entered the court room to see it festooned with balloons and party decorations. They were left in the hall from a dance which had been held the previous evening. The judge decreed that it was not right to hold dances in what doubled as a court.

Peter Sellers and Britt Ekland's wedding

Were you among the crowd of 500 people who gathered outside Guildford Register Office on 18 February 1964 to catch a glimpse of actor Peter Sellers and his Swedish bride Britt Ekland.

It was a rather dark winter's day with light snow falling. But it was the place to be for both film fans and fans of *The Goon Show*, plus other well-wishers who waited patiently for the 38-year-old Sellers's maroon Lincoln car to arrive.

Shortly afterwards his 21-year-old bride-to-be arrived with her parents in a coffee and black coloured Rolls-Royce.

The register office at Artington House, off Portsmouth Road, was transformed into a haven of soft light, lit by about 50 candles in the Swedish tradition, and scented by lilies and roses.

The 15-minute ceremony was directed by the superintendent registrar, George Catt, assisted by Mrs P.J. Barber, the registrar of marriages.

George Catt politely told 'Inspector Clouseau' that he could not sign the register with his own gold fountain pen, but had to use the official pen with its permanent black ink.

A *Surrey Advertiser* reporter was the only member of the press who sat in on the ceremony. The reporter wrote: 'After the ceremony, Mr Catt congratulated the couple. He welcomed Miss Ekland to England on behalf of the people of Guildford and said he hoped she would enjoy living in the beautiful Surrey countryside.'

The newspaper also reported that Miss Ekland's wedding dress was a short wild silk gown from Norman Hartnell. Her long blonde hair was piled under a pillbox hat of silk flowers. Similar silk 'fantasy' flowers bordered the hem of her dress. She carried a Victorian posy of pink roses and lily-of-the-valley.

After the ceremony, other members of the press were allowed in to interview the couple. Evidently, Peter Sellers looked nervous and said little, while his bride beamed radiantly. Photographers then jostled to get images of the couple for the daily newspapers.

So dense was the crowd outside – which the *Surrey Advertiser* stated was made up of shop-girls, office workers and a sprinkling of older women and some men – that it took Mr Sellers' chauffeur, Bert Mortimer (also his best man), 10 minutes to drive the wedding car the short distance from the register office to the Portsmouth Road. Four policeman walked in front while more photographers lined the drive, either positioned on a wall or up trees.

The couple returned to the actor's 16th-century cottage, Brookfield, at Elstead, for a champagne and smorgasbord reception. Here there were more well-wishers and the new Mrs Sellers was seen wearing a mink coat that her husband had given her as a wedding gift. She had bought him a watch.

Peter Sellers's nine-year-old son Michael, from his 10-year marriage to Anne Howe, obliged villagers by standing at the cottage gate selling pieces of wedding cake for sixpence a time.

An evening reception was spent in Mayfair, at the Tiberio Terrazza Restaurant, before the couple departed for their honeymoon in Jamaica.

Fifty days after the much publicised wedding, Peter Sellers suffered his second heart attack while working on a new film in Hollywood. So distraught was his new bride that she left the set of her own film, *Guns of Batasi*, only to be sued by 20th Century Fox for £535,000.

There was a break-in at the couple's Elstead home in 1965, in which a seal-skin coat belonging to Britt was taken, along with a pair of Dresden ornaments. Evidently, Mr Sellers was at home when the burglary took place.

Within three years, the couple had moved away from Elstead, and, in 1968, they divorced.

Peter Sellers was a talented and much-loved actor. He was married twice more (to Miranda Quarry and Lynne Frederick) and died after another heart attack in 1980. His ashes were scattered at Golders Green Crematorium. One of his wishes was that the song *In The Mood* be played at his funeral. This was a final joke on Sellers' part, as most of his friends knew that he hated the song.

The *Surrey Advertiser's* report in words and pictures of the wedding of Peter Sellers and Britt Ekland at Guildford Register Office in 1964.

A few of the hundreds of congratulatory smiles surrounded the bridal car as it left Guildford Office. Other special pictures of the wedding in a late edition of the 'Guildford and Godalming Advertiser' on Wednesday.

Peter Sellers and the new Mrs. Sellers ignore the offer of an umbrella to wave to well-wishers outside Mr. Sellers' Elstead house, where the reception was held.
[Photo: Studio 57]

The wedding with more than 500 'guests'

Sixties ice age

'A week of crazy mixed-up weather creates a dizzy dilemma' ran the headline on the front page of the *Guildford & Godalming Times* on Saturday 5 January 1963.

The effects of the heavy snow that had fallen on the UK were certainly being felt in Guildford. The newspaper report began: 'In yesterday's bright sunshine Guildford wore the air of a Swiss holiday resort. It was the climax of a week of crazy weather – snow, thaw, frost, thaw, slush, rain, snow, thaw, fog, through which Guildfordians sloshed and slithered. It was a week of digging-out, worrying about milk, bread and coal deliveries… and of the irrepressible good humour of the great British public when in trouble.'

Global warming and its effects were unheard of during the harsh winter of late 1962 and early 1963. It was like a mini Ice Age!

Christmas Day saw the normal indifferent winter weather, but on Boxing Day night it started to snow. There was some disappointment that this was too late for a white Christmas, but by New Year's Eve many roads were closed due to snow drifts, and the emergency services, under-strength for the festive season, were struggling to rescue people who were stranded.

The snow continued to fall over the following weeks, and the big freeze set in which lasted until the middle of March.

That first issue of the *Guildford & Godalming Times* for 1963 also reported that milkmen were having a particularly hard time making their rounds. One, from Mead's dairy in Shalford, started his round at 5am in the morning and didn't get back until 8.30pm. He then had to make his way back to his home in Cline Road, Guildford.

The following week's newspaper reported the story of an Aldershot & District double-decker bus travelling from Farnham to Guildford that skidded off the road near Normandy. Four of the 40 passengers were slightly injured and were taken to the Royal Surrey County Hospital in Farnham Road.

Workers in the building trade were particularly hard hit. By the middle of January, the Guildford Labour Exchange said that up to 200 workers had been stood off. A spokesperson said that if the cold weather continued that figure would rise substantially.

An unofficial go-slow by workers at Guildford power station meant that lower incoming voltage resulted in homes and businesses suffering dimmer lights, electric fires with less heat and in some cases bad television pictures.

A bride was left with no choice but to cancel her wedding reception for a second time because of the bad weather. Winifred Brown had trudged through deep snow to marry Captain Stanley Brown at Guildford Register Office. However, guests, including their best man and bridesmaids, failed to make it. She told the *Guildford & Godalming Times*: 'We decided to have the reception on Sunday,

Thick snow in Guildford High Street during the 'sixties Ice Age'.

but again it was impossible because of the weather. At least my husband will not go short of food. We have a giant turkey, pounds of ham, scores of sausages and lots of cakes.'

At weekends people flocked to Shalford Park to skate on the ice on the flooded meadows. The borough charged sixpence a time and the attendant, Philip Dance, said that more than 1,000 people had been there on each of the first two Sundays in January.

Although there was much sympathy for milkmen, postmen, newspaper boys and so on,

Put it on ice! These people are enjoying drinks on the frozen River Wey outside the Jolly Farmer pub.

Get your skates on! Youngsters try out the ice on the frozen river between Millmead and Shalford Park.

few would have given a thought to the difficulty grave-diggers were having. The sexton at St Mary's Church in Worplesdon, Cliff Heather, was having to pick-axe his way through five inches of frozen soil before he could begin to dig properly. He told Les Bromley of the *Guildford & Godalming Times* that he had struggled to dig six graves since Christmas. The pile of soil from each hole then froze solid and could not be replaced after the burials.

More blizzards struck in the first week of February, closing the Guildford to Leatherhead road between Merrow and West Horsley for two days.

At one point during this cold winter, the gritting of roads was stopped so as to save reserves for further fresh snowfalls. Breeze, a mixture of ash and sand, was sometimes used.

The frozen ice and snow at the sides of the roads took on a grimy look, until refreshed by further heavy snow falls. Pathways and pavements became narrow, so travelling on foot was sometimes as difficult as driving motor vehicles.

Snow falling on stocks of coal that had frozen hard meant that it was difficult for coal merchants to dig it out. The *Surrey Advertiser* received many letters from disgruntled readers who had run out of coal. The local coal merchants responded with tales of machinery in the yard that had frozen up, as well as axles of railway coal trucks freezing.

The chairman of the Guildford and District Coal Merchants' Association, Mr R.H. Franks, said that quantities of inferior coals such as Yorkshire Small Nuts and Industrial Singles could be available at one shilling a ton.

Radiators of buses and lorries split as diesel oil froze. Few vehicles used anti-freeze, so radiators had to be drained each night. Failure to cover the radiator grills during the day could cause the pipework to freeze, even when the vehicle was in motion. The water would not circulate properly and would therefore start to boil. Motorists had to wait at the side of the road for the boiling water to melt the ice at the bottom of the radiator before topping up the system.

In the home everyone was cold. Extra blankets were piled on to beds with little relief from the sub-zero temperatures.

Few people had central heating, and the lagging of pipes, water tanks and lofts was not common either. For those who had these luxuries, it was something of a status symbol to see snow melting on your roof while other householders not so well off had to endure snow-covered roofs for weeks. Plumbers had their work cut out calling on countless homes with frozen pipes. The work involved crawling around extremely cold roof spaces, thawing out the pipes with a blowlamp.

The Women's Royal Voluntary Service, despite the weather, did not lose a single day in their meals-on-wheels service. They issued between 60 and 70 meals, three days a week, as well as running a mobile library.

Across the frozen river to Shalford Park where people are skating.

Livestock suffered and so did wildlife. Foxes were seen foraging for food in built-up parts of the borough. Some foxes, it was reported, were forced to hunt like a pack of wolves.

On Saturday 23 March 1963, the *Guildford & Godalming Times* reported that 'the iron grip of winter has given way at last to the velvet touch of spring'.

It also reported that a team of three shire horses had been tackling spring harrowing at Secretts farm in Milford, and that daily life for people in and around Guildford had finally got back to normal.

1968 floods

Floods on a scale that were reckoned to occur only once every 1,000 years brought chaos to Guildford in September 1968.

Heavy rain began to fall on the night of Saturday 14 September, continuing unabated the next day. That evening, water began seeping into homes and premises beside the River Wey near the town

The floods around Plummers in Millbrook.

When water began to lap around the vestry door of St Nicolas' Church near the Town Bridge, the rector, the Revd W. Goddard, and helpers, moved vestments on to the high altar. However, when it was realised that the water was getting higher, valuable items, including a 17th-century chalice, were taken out to a boat moored by the churchyard wall and ferried to safety. The rector described witnessing a small tidal wave going down the nave.

Early on the Monday morning, staff at the Yvonne Arnaud Theatre were able to move scenery from the stage to safety. Then the waters rose and completely covered the stage and about 100 seats in the auditorium. It receded the next day, but much damage had been done.

At the printers Billings, in Walnut Tree Close, all its bound stock, flat sheets and printed white paper had to be thrown out. By the Wednesday afternoon the pile of rubbish outside had grown to about 20 yards long and 10 feet wide.

Next door, at the premises of Franks, Harris & Co. a 300-gallon oil tank burst, spilling its contents into the river.

There was no shortage of willing volunteers to help with the clear-up operation. These included girls from the Women's Royal Army Corps Camp at Stoughton, the Red Cross, the Women's Royal Voluntary Service and local Scouts and Guides. The town clerk, Herbert Weller, said that the first task was to clean and dry the 150 flooded homes.

Canoeing down Friary Street.

This view of the 1968 floods is likely to have been taken from Bridge House. The houses in Bedford Road are in the foreground with the gas holders beyond.

William Road suffered as a result of the River Wey bursting its banks.

Supt J.M. Packham of Guildford Police said that the floods became an emergency on the Sunday when it was found that within a short time the main roads to London were blocked. These included the A3 at Send, the A321 at Worplesdon, and the A320 at Jacob's Well. Traffic converged at the AA roundabout at the top of Stoke Park, and although there was floodwater there, the road was passable, but it was very congested.

The police had several calls to evacuate people from houses along the River Wey. They were rescued in police and army inflatable dinghies and taken to Sandfield Terrace Drill Hall, where at one time 250 people were accommodated.

At his home in Guildford, amateur

Water laps around the Bridge Café in Ladymead, opposite Woodbridge Road.

The River Wey also burst its banks and flooded Woodbridge Road at the junction with Ladymead. A policeman keeps an eye on the traffic as it slowly passes.

A recovery vehicle and a lorry make their way along Ladymead.

meteorologist Dennis Mullen recorded 3.75in of rain on the Sunday. A water board spokesman said that statistically the scale of the flood could only happen once in 1,000 years.

The then Mayor of Guildford, Alderman J.B. O'Keefe, said: 'I think the town should be pleased by the way they have been served by our services. When the full story is told there will be credit due to a lot of people.'

A fund was set up to help those who had suffered and the mayor urged people who had not been affected to contribute.

The High Street was closed to through traffic on the Sunday night and the Monday, when the flood water was at its highest. However, it was strange to see people still pressing the button on the pedestrian crossings and waiting until the sign indicated it was safe to cross! The manager of the Yvonne Arnaud Theatre, Gordon Marshall, claimed he was the only person held up in a rowing boat by the pedestrian crossing in Millbrook!

BIBLIOGRAPHY

Colin Buchanan & Partners website. Available from: www.cbuchanan.co.uk

Collyer, Graham and David Rose *Images of Guildford* Breedon Books, 1998.

Collyer, Graham and David Rose *Guildford The War Years 1939–45* Breedon Books, 1999.

Drummonds Bros Ltd, a pamphlet issued by Guildford Museum.

Guildford A Residential Centre, Corporation of Guildford, 1939 edition.

Guildford & Godalming Times

Hilderley, Janet *Yvonne Arnaud a biography* self-published, 2006.

Mee, Arthur *The King's England Surrey* The King's England Press, 2001 reprint of the 1938 edition.

NewCriminologist online edition website. Available from: www.newcriminologist.com

NHS in England website. Available from: www.nhs.uk

Oakley, W.H. *Guildford In The Great War* Billings & Sons Ltd, Guildford, 1934.

Parker, Malcolm *The Viper Gazette* Website that contains a section about Victory Industries of Guildford. Available from: www.madmalc.screaming.net/index.html

Rose, David *The Building Of St Clare's Church* Parish of Westborough and Park Barn, 2003.

Rose, David *Memory Lane Guildford & District* Breedon Books, 2000.

Surrey Advertiser & County Times

Surrey Times

Wikipedia. Available from: www.wikipedia.org

Wonderful Life – The Good Fortune of Nigel Vinson Courtesey of Lord Vinson.

Worplesdon 2000 The Tale of Four Villages Published by Worplesdon Parish Council, 2000.

Yvonne Arnaud Theatre Trust newsletter-brochure, 1963.

Yvonne Arnaud Theatre opening festival programme, 1965.

Yvonne Arnaud Theatre opening supplement published by the *Surrey Advertiser*, June 1965.